A COUNTRY
AT WAR
WITH ITSELF

For Jackie, Mia and Ben
More than just pretty screensavers

A COUNTRY AT WAR WITH ITSELF

South Africa's crisis of crime

Antony Altbeker

JONATHAN BALL PUBLISHERS

JOHANNESBURG & CAPE TOWN

Published in 2007 by
JONATHAN BALL PUBLISHERS (PTY) LTD
PO Box 33977
Jeppestown
2043

Reprinted 2007
Reprinted 2008

ISBN 978-1-86842-284-5

Cover design and reproduction by Mr Design, Cape Town
Typesetting and reproduction of text by Alinea Studio, Cape Town
Printed and bound by CTP Book Printers, Cape Town

CONTENTS

ACKNOWLEDGEMENTS

In writing this book, I have drawn on the research and ideas of a number of people who have thought hard about crime and policing in South Africa. I have no doubt that none of them would endorse everything I have written and some would actively disown it. Nevertheless, I owe a debt of gratitude to many. I cannot put a name to every thought in the book, but some of the more important ideas have ripened in the course of conversations with my colleagues and friends, Jonny Steinberg, Janine Rauch, Antoinette Louw, David Bruce and Boyane Tshehla.

My thanks are also owed to Frances Perryer and Valda Strauss for their editorial assistance, as well as to Jeremy Borraine and Jonathan Ball at Jonathan Ball Publishers for betting on this book.

Man never understands that the cities he has built are not an integral part of Nature. If he wants to defend his culture from wolves and snowstorms, if he wants to save it from being strangled by weeds, he must sleep with his broom, spade and rifle always at hand. If he goes to sleep, if he thinks about something else for a year or two, then everything's lost. The wolves come out of the forest, the thistles spread and everything is buried under dust and snow. Just think how many great capitals have succumbed to dust, snow and couch-grass.

Life and Fate, Vasily Grossman

PREFACE

For a democracy, South Africa's relationship to crime is an odd one.

In most democratic countries, when the populace is convinced that it is living through a crime wave of heart-stopping proportions, its government not only acknowledges the crisis, but takes advantage of public panic to write new laws onto the books, in the process granting itself increasingly robust, sometimes sinister powers. Public fear, from this point of view, is a godsend for an authoritarian-streaked politician: 'You want safety?' he asks. 'Well, this is what it takes …' This has been the case in the United States with its ill-starred wars on drugs and terror. Margaret Thatcher's remaking of Britain was also based, in part, on the construction of a law-and-order constituency whose fear of street crime had been whipped up by Maggie's foot soldiers in the tabloid press. Having brought the Tories to power, these voters consented to the rewriting of the social contract in return for all the red meat thrown to them in the form of more aggressive policing and more punitive sentencing.

By these lights, our government has missed a tremendous opportunity to augment its powers. Instead of actively using public fear to its own advantage, it has done the opposite, pooh-poohing dismay as irrational and perhaps even racist in origin. 'Don't panic,' is its endlessly repeated message, expressed, generally, in a tone of benign, resigned wisdom.

To prove government's case, critics are told to look more closely at the country's crime stats. There, they are told, they will see that murder rates have fallen quickly since the mid-1990s, as have rates of car theft and burglary (though from a slightly later date). Rates of non-lethal violence – rape and assault and attempted murder – while not much lower than they were, are also no worse than a decade ago and have retreated from the peaks of a few years ago. Then there are our crowded prisons and the growing number of police officers on the streets: these, we are told, are not the signs of a government ignoring the problem of crime.

Frustratingly, though, government has found that its message has not gained much traction with the public, with surveys consistently showing that levels of fear are up and that crime ranks as one of the country's most pressing concerns. In the face of this, the insistence that the stats are improving, instead of reassuring the public, has fuelled scepticism about government honesty. And about its ability to remake the country.

This is not without reason because, whatever the improvement in some crime rates since 1994 and however sincerely government believes its claims, the unavoidable, irreducible reality is that every single piece of reliable data we have tells us that South Africa ranks at the very top of the world's league tables for violent crime. It is true that some data from countries in the developing world are patchy. But none that I have ever seen has suggested anything other than that we are an exceptionally, possibly uniquely, violent society.

12

It is the disjuncture between this and the sense that no outrage can penetrate the cloud of wilful optimism that hovers around our politicians, that has convinced many that government has tortured its crime stats to make them jump up and sing. For many, it is as if government has become resigned to tragedy, inured to the way it shapes people's lives, and has chosen instead to spin a tale of sunshine and light.

I will say more about all this, but it may be that something even more troubling is going on here: I suspect that if government had solutions to our crime problems in its policy toolbox – whether these involved sinister new police powers or not – I'm pretty sure it would both acknowledge the depth of the crime wave and, simultaneously, act decisively to end it. It may be, in other words, that government is not heartlessly out of touch with the plight of its people, but that it is out of ideas; its denialism may be more a symptom of its inability to roll back the crime wave than its cause.

That government may have run out of crime-fighting ideas is a disturbing thought, but not a surprising one. The roots of our crime problems run deep and the arsenal of tools available to government – to any government – are not exactly overflowing with silver bullets. This is not because policy-makers are stupid, uninterested or ill-intentioned, but because our crime problems really are that intractable.

Finding solutions has not been made any easier, however, by what has happened to the various levels of public debate about crime.

One level of this debate – that which takes place in parliament, at dinner tables and on the airwaves – has become so highly charged and politicised that, for all the heat generated, little light will ever emerge. Among criminal justice policy-makers and researchers, on the other hand, a grey, somewhat complacent consensus has descended. Government officials, members of the NGO community, academia and the serious-minded pundit-ocracy of the press all share common assumptions about the causes of crime as well as about the purpose, quality and effectiveness of policing. They also share an ingrained conviction that it is somehow unpatriotic to differ publicly with the official line.

This book is a reaction to both levels of public discourse. It is an essay on the causes of crime and the nature of our response to it based on 13 years of work in and around the criminal justice system. It is deliberately polemic and, in some areas, provocative. It is not, however, political in the sense of its being partisan. Unlike many of the studiously sober contributions to this field, it tries to show that public fears are not irrational, that they have a tragically firm basis in reality: our crime problems really are that bad. At the same time, those who think that getting on top of crime is merely a matter of political will or technical competence, will find that their views are also challenged in the pages that follow.

At the level of policy debate, the book is an extended argument against the consensus that reigns in the crime prevention policy community about the causes of crime, the suitability and appropriateness of our policies on policing and criminal justice, and the need to find alternatives to prison rather than build more of them.

Making South Africa safer is one of the great challenges government faces. Whether this ought to rank above or

below our many other problems – poverty, AIDS, inadequate housing, and the rest – is a question about which
reasonable people can disagree. Getting our response to
crime right, however, demands a far better understanding
of the nature of the problem. That, in turn, requires more
informed, more rigorous public discussion about what to
do. No doubt, many of my friends and colleagues in government, the police and in NGOs will disagree with a
good deal of what follows. Whatever their reaction, the
book you hold in your hands was written in the not-so-
humble hope that a better-informed public will lead to
better policy-making.

CHAPTER ONE

'STUFF HAPPENS' OR HOW WE USED TO THINK ABOUT CRIME

There can be few South Africans who have yet to become a crime statistic. In our divided land, it is the one experience we have all shared. Whether it's a mugging or a hijacking, the burglary of one's home or a rape, a moment of high drama in a shopping centre or the banality of a stolen car, we all have a story to tell. Mine is of a restaurant robbery in 1997.

*

On a winter's evening in the middle of 1997, I was eating steak rolls with *slap* chips in one of Johannesburg's franchised fast-food emporia with a friend. I had my back to the room, and my companion, Angela, a fey, hippy-ish blonde who also happens to have a fine head for figures, was sitting in the corner. About halfway through the meal a figure appeared at the side of our table. Dressed in jeans and a rugby shirt, he was short and young – no more than 16 or 17, possibly younger. With a hesitation that verged on timidity, he showed us the top of the barrel of a handgun and told us to get down.

Now, it is no embarrassment to me to admit that I have

no gun sense. I don't know a .22 from a .45, a pistol from a revolver; I don't know a cheap Chinese import from a Cold War-era Makarov. Something about this would-be robber's tone of voice, his body language and the cautious way he showed only the top of the gun, however, made me suspicious. He reminded me of a classmate at school who, with exaggerated, implausible stealth, pulled me aside one afternoon and, seeking to profit from my pharmacological naiveté, offered me a bottle of Vitamin E pills, claiming they were LSD tabs. I had the same thought now as I had then: 'This is not real.' In the restaurant this thought was followed by another: 'This prick is threatening me with a toy!'

'Fuck off,' I said, allowing the tartrazine in the mustard to get the better of me. 'Go away.'

'Get down,' the boy-man repeated. There was astonishment in his voice, and he began to raise the weapon towards my face.

'It's a fucking toy,' I said to Angela, getting up, rage boiling in my breast and reducing my vocabulary to four-letter words. 'I'm going to fuck this little shit up.' Turning on him, I struck his wrist with my left hand, knocking the gun away from me. Then I hit him in the neck, just above the breastbone.

I am not a big man, though I am tall. Skinny to the point of frailty, my legs, for instance, cast a shadow only when I wear dark trousers. Still, I played schoolboy rugby until I was about 14 largely because, beanpole though I was, I could tackle. So, visions of Henry Honiball dancing in my head, I pursued the little man I had just punched as he staggered backwards into the restaurant. I was going to *donner* him into the ground.

As I was about to pounce, his friend put a gun in my face.

No doubt others have had this experience, and perhaps they can relate to the sensation of time slowing down precipitously, its flow congealing like day-old toffee. I was in hot pursuit, about to leap on fleeing prey, about to turn a would-be robber into the next victim of vigilantism, when the universal clock simply stopped. It gave me what seemed to be a surprising length of time in which to contemplate my immediate future. I can't have had more than half a second to think these thoughts, but this is what went through my head:

'Item: the boy-man's gun didn't go off. Even though I've hit his arm. Even though I've hit him in the neck. Even though I'm still threatening him.

'Conclusion: his gun *must* be a toy.

'Item: this new fellow knows that I am being aggressive. He knows that he needs to gain control over me. He knows that I am idiot enough to resist him. Nevertheless, he is choosing to threaten me with his gun.

'Conclusion: *his* gun must be real.'

I stopped and put both hands in the air.

'Back to the table.' He gestured with his weapon rather than spoke, but I did as I was told.

The second man, the man with the real gun, was also small, but he was older than the first. Despite the cold, his shirt had no sleeves and his muscles looked as hard and raw as tendons. He wore a skullcap made of thinly-striped blue cloth that framed a narrow, strangely reddish face with high cheekbones and that came to the sharpest, pointiest chin I have ever seen. I remember all of this because, while the teenager who'd first threatened me looted the cash register

19

and demanded wallets from the restaurant's staff and its other patrons, Pointy Face and I had a long conversation. The gist of our deliberations was that I was mad and should be dead. I could, in truth, appreciate the point.

I was conscious of trying not to be too conciliatory or to seem to be telling him how to do his job, but I was also trying to assure him that I had learned my lesson. 'Take what you want,' I kept saying. 'No-one has to get hurt.' I was hyper-aware of two things. The first was that my actions had made it more likely that someone in the room would get hurt; Angela, who was directly behind me and in the path of any bullets that might pass through my skinny torso, was especially at risk. The second was a flash of insight: if I could get this bastard to see me as a human being rather than a mere wallet-carrier, he would be less likely to shoot. If he were to see me as anything less than a human, though, I'd be dead. Both thoughts led to one conclusion: I had to engage him. I knew with unnatural clarity that I had to maintain eye contact. I had to speak to him.

In defiance of the objective facts, that insight made me feel in full control.

Pointy Face wanted my jacket; I gave it to him. He wanted my cellphone; I gave that to him, too, vaguely conscious that it was the property of the Ministry for Safety and Security. Then he wanted my wallet.

I was buggered if he was going to get my credit cards and my name. Instead, I took the wallet out of my pocket, emptied the cash, handed him the notes, and put it back in my pocket. I worried while I did this, fearing that I may be offending his sense of dignity and position. He felt this too, I think, and for a moment I imagined he was considering demanding the rest of the wallet's contents. But perhaps I was wrong. Perhaps Pointy Face was too self-conscious to ask for more. Perhaps he felt his authority wane as mine increased. In any event, he didn't ask for anything that had my name on it.

My interaction with Pointy Face must have lasted five minutes, the most dangerous moment coming towards the end of that period when a woman, another would-be burger-eater like myself, another wallet-carrier, entered the restaurant and walked straight into him. Panicking as she realised what was happening, she tried to retreat out of the door. Pointy Face was quicker. Grabbing her by the arm, he pulled her into the room, the momentum carrying her off her feet. The distraction upset the flow between Pointy Face and me and, when he looked up, he announced matter-of-factly that he was going to kill me. His voice was cool, with a hint of something like resentment that I had brought matters to this. Nevertheless, it was, he felt, imperative that he shoot me.

As he spoke, he moved to cock the gun.

This is a matter I have since discussed with a number of police officers of my acquaintance and each has been clear on this point: if someone cocks his gun, he is planning to shoot. Up until that moment, a robbery victim's best bet, they insist, is to cooperate fully. But everything changes when a bullet has been chambered and the gun has been cocked. When that happens, whatever the circumstances, however great your disadvantage, you have to act. 'You've got to attack,' one policewoman told me. 'If you don't, you're going home in the mortuary van.'

This is something I now know because cops have told

21

me. But, even at the time, I remember contemplating the option of launching myself at this man who'd walked out of the night, stolen my jacket and money and phone, and who was now threatening to end my life. The trouble was that there was a table between us; there was just no way to get at him.

For a moment, I knew I was going to die.

This was a hard, physical piece of wisdom, one that left imprinted on my mind a picture, almost a sensation, of the blunt, shattering violence that would be delivered by a bullet to so brittle a structure as a human skull.

My skull.

Even now it makes my stomach turn.

As if I had not already had my share of good fortune that evening, what happened next suggested that I should have gone straight to a casino: the gun's mechanism jammed; it couldn't be cocked.

Pointy Face tried only once, but somehow I knew he didn't have it in him to risk failing again. I had the impression of a workman embarrassed by the failure of his tools.

As quickly as the knowledge that I was going to die passed through my body, so it was replaced by the elation that I would live. For that moment, I loved Pointy Face, and I contemplated a joke. 'I know,' I was going to say with faked solicitousness, 'that you're just doing your job.' Then I thought again. This guy's not on my Christmas card list; I don't have to be his friend. Barely had these two thoughts flashed through my head than he used the same words to me: 'I'm just doing my job,' he said, as if hoping for greater understanding of, and sympathy for, his position.

'Bingo,' I thought. 'We've bonded; I've become a human being.'

And then, just as suddenly as it had begun, it was over: my new best friend was gone and the aftermath began. Someone cried. Someone started mixing sugar water for the shock. A third person called the cops. Angela, I discovered later, was deciding never to speak to me again. I smoked a cigarette and talked to a man who turned out to be a champion boxer. Even he thought I was an idiot.

Dazedly we sat in a room, violated and relieved, a stunned rabble in a room of overturned chairs.

Never let it be said, though, that Johannesburg's finest weren't there when we needed them. It couldn't have been ten minutes later when two cops arrived, automatic weapons draped over their shoulders. Boldly, confident in their authority, they walked in and looked at us.

Silently, we returned their gaze.

They looked at the menu.

'Are you here for the robbery?' I asked, puzzled.

'What robbery?' the sergeant replied.

They'd come in for supper. Fifteen minutes earlier and we'd have been players in a hostage drama.

*

The night I spent with Pointy Face took place in mid-1997, a time when I was working for the Minister for Safety and Security. In a job like that you are accorded some advantages that others are denied. One was that I could spend the next day berating the Minister, demanding from him some explanation of what exactly it was he thought he and his department were doing to solve the crime problem. I think I suggested that he get out of his office more.

He humoured me politely.

Another privilege I had was that, when I expressed my disbelief to the investigating officer that the first appointment I could make with the only remaining police identikit artist was a week after the robbery, I was quickly offered an earlier slot. I refused it, but was troubled by the thought that in the two years I'd worked for the Minister reviewing police expenditure trends and budget submissions, perhaps we had not taken seriously enough the operational impact of the loss of skills the organisation was suffering. Having inherited something like 145 000 cops in 1994 – the number is imprecise because of the many ghost employees on Bantustan payrolls – by the time I met Pointy Face in mid-1997, the Police Service employed fewer than 130 000.

The loss of personnel, damaging enough, coincided with a massively destabilising programme of organisational transformation and reform as well as an explosion of crime. All this had devastated police morale. White cops, especially in middle and senior ranks, having accumulated the lion's share of skills under apartheid, were now taking advantage of government's generous severance packages, clearing their desks and finding other things to do with the rest of their lives. I knew that this was the organisational context, but the idea that it would be a week before I could sit with a police artist was worrying: criminological studies everywhere show that witnesses' ability to describe a suspect, weak at the best of times, decays rapidly as their memories falter. What else, I wondered, didn't I know about how transformation was affecting police operations?

I was not alone in my obliviousness about the operational consequences of the loss of personnel. If I'd asked them at the time, my colleagues in the Ministry would have offered our boilerplate response that these were the inevitable short-term costs of a transformation process that would improve policing in the medium and long term. 'Besides,' my hypothetical interlocutor would have said, 'the skills of those who are leaving are not relevant to a police service operating in a democracy and guided by the philosophy of community policing. Especially in a country as diverse as ours.'

Our eye, we said (and sincerely believed), was on the long term.

Senior leadership in police headquarters was not necessarily any better at looking after the health of the organisation than were we, the left-wing civilians sitting in the Minister's boardroom. Mole-blind, at the nominal helm of an institution that is too unwieldy to control from the centre, they were just as badly out of touch.

They also had a lot on their plate.

Apart from the wave of panic about crime that was beginning to sweep through post-liberation South Africa, apart from their having to preside over one of the most dramatic processes of police reform ever contemplated, apart from the loss of skills and the decline in morale, apart from all this, they were also having to figure out how to secure their own futures in a new, unfamiliar government whose politics and policies might as well have originated on Jupiter. No wonder they were out of touch. No wonder none but the boldest would offer anything more than token protest, offered sometimes for form's sake alone, when they believed any new policies were impacting negatively on police effectiveness. Besides, most had been head-office desk-jockeys for so long, they had almost no sense of what policing South Africa's streets was like. Or how quickly it was changing.

★

From early colonial times, policing in South Africa had been dominated by a conviction that the whole social order rested on the vigorous application of force against anyone deemed a threat. Political resistance was one kind of threat, but so too was criminality, much of which was inseparable from the underlying ethos of resistance. In the 19th century, for instance, local magistrates would lead posses of burghers out beyond the boundaries of the colony to hunt down cattle thieves, operations that were integral to the conflicts between settler and indigene that marked the growth of the colony. The first detective units worked the diamond fields of Kimberley, emerging at the same time and for the same reason as the building of the first mine hostels: the reduction of illegal diamond dealing. Later, in the 20th century, policing was more concerned with reinforcing the racial social structure than with preventing crime. Indeed, for most cops, the two objectives would have been indistinguishable since they routinely served in the townships combating mass resistance to apartheid, fought in Namibia to prevent its independence, and even waged counter-insurgency warfare in what was then Rhodesia. Who can blame the young men involved for thinking that policing and maintaining the political order were one in the same thing? For all practical purposes, they were.

Given this history, it was hardly surprising that much of the transformational effort immediately after 1994 was directed at reining in police abuses, a process that was sometimes understood to mean the reining in of policing more generally. Anti-torture policies were adopted and human-rights training was initiated. Police watchdogs – the Independent Complaints Directorate and the Secretariats for Safety and Security – were established. Kicking and screaming, cops were dragged to the Truth Commission. An aggressive programme of demilitarisation sought to change police culture, structures and symbols. At the same time, new rules governing the right to bail made it significantly easier for arrestees to obtain their release, others narrowed sharply the circumstances under which officers could legally fire their weapons. The unrelated decision of the Constitutional Court that the death penalty offended against the right to life, handed down around that time, implied to cops – pro-death penalty to a man – that government envisaged a softer approach to the enforcement of the law.

Along with all these changes, a new model of policing was being aggressively pursued. Based on faddish notions of community policing and crime prevention drawn from the pages of international criminology journals, it was premised on a conviction that traditional police methods for tackling crime were ineffective. It was argued that the existing approach – contemptuously called the 'professional model of policing' – resulted in policing that was too remote, too isolated from the community to deal with the social problems that gave rise to crime. Instead, the police were to

27

embed themselves in communities and become the fulcrum about which social transformation would turn.

You might think that when a new model of policing – of police officer – is needed, a police service would go out to recruit people to fill the new job descriptions. You might think that but, at least in our case, you'd be wrong. In fact, in the midst of all of this destabilising change, in the midst of the fastest rising crime wave since at least the Anglo-Boer War, a moratorium was imposed on police recruitment. It was the result of budget constraints attendant on rising police salaries rather than a deliberate policy choice to shrink police numbers, but it also went unregretted and unprotested by people in key policy positions.

The effort to introduce a new model of policing while watching police personnel numbers shrink was, I now believe, a symptom of one of the most striking aspects of the manner in which reform was being managed: the process was almost entirely driven by the abstractions of policy rather than the operational questions of what it would take to provide decent policing. Papers were passed from one office at police headquarters to the next. They were read, parsed and criticised. Then they were sent back. It was like an enormous game of pass-the-parcel, and it only very occasionally involved anyone working outside the bureau-cratic towers in the middle of Pretoria. What was going on in the street – that was for others to worry about.

For the 'blokes on ground level', as one senior cop took to calling them, the lunatics were running the asylum; everything that came out of the policy process smacked of an unarticulated contempt for law enforcement and, by extension, for law enforcers. (Nor were they necessarily wrong. I remember a conversation with some of the Minister's advisors in 1995 when a call had gone out to institute a state of emergency in the battlefields of KwaZulu-Natal. When I asked why everyone was opposed to it, I was told that sending thousands of 'useless police-men' to the province would achieve nothing. Whether this was true or not, the idea of the 'useless policeman' took hold among members of the policy-making community who hover around the criminal justice system like gawkers at the scene of a car accident.)

True believers in their craft, thousands of cops, good and bad, were bewildered by the range and aggressiveness of the changes that were being made. They picked up a sense that their new bosses saw policing as one of the country's prob-lems, not one of its most essential services. More so because what they were seeing on the streets was scaring the be-jesus out of them. 'Don't they get it?' one asked me in 1998 after I'd left the ministry. 'How can they tear up all the umbrellas just as a storm is breaking?'

*

Police officers, of course, weren't the only ones concerned about the rise in crime; so too were the public, for whom the Byzantine politics of police transformation were opa-que, inexplicable and largely irrelevant. Despite the crime wave, though, there was a surprising amount of patience with government in the first four or five years after the inauguration of democracy. Most people understood that criminality was a complex challenge and that it was un-realistic to expect a new government to find and then flip a switch that would throw the problem into reverse; they knew there was no such switch. Government's view, articulated at every opportunity, was not just that the law enforcement machinery it had inherited was ill-suited to the task of reducing crime, but that the whole idea that a criminal justice system could make South Africa safer was flawed. Crime, government believed, was not something that could be addressed through what was called, in the oh-so-superior language of the global crime prevention community, 'bandit catching'. It required, instead, an integrated programme of fundamental social re-ordering.

The attractions and seductions this kind of thinking would have had for a post-liberation government are obvious. It asserted, for one, the essential goodness of the people, and assigned the blame for the darker traits in the national character to the legacies of the hated policies of the past. Better still, it reinforced an instinctive left-of-centre politics which held that the socio-economic upliftment of communities would lead to the withering away of crime. Crucially, it was also essentially true: apartheid, an extreme, long-lived experiment in social engineering that shaped and deformed society for two generations, really was responsible for the cruelties people suffered and, therefore, for their subsequent behaviour. Because the crime wave was a symptom of the deformities in our social order, the effect of causes that lay in the nature of the society it had inherited, government didn't and couldn't see criminal justice as the solution. As a consequence law enforcement was seen as a much lower priority than the RDP's efforts aimed at ameliorating the structural problems of poverty and unemployment. People will be safer, the argument went, only when the causes of crime are addressed.

Even if all this was true, crime in post-liberation South Africa quickly became a hot political problem and, as public fears grew, it became increasingly difficult to sell a root-causes-first argument. The honeymoon ended quickly and, by the late 1990s, the apparent wisdom of government's conviction that crime had its roots in social problems that must be tackled first, began to sound like a refusal to take responsibility for the problem. For some, it would not have sounded all that different from the callous indifference Donald Rumsfeld would later show in response to the looting that took place in Baghdad after the invasion in 2003: 'Stuff happens,' he said. 'Freedom is messy.'

Recognising that its argument about crime was becoming increasingly unpersuasive, government began to change tack. This change was personified by a Cabinet reshuffle which saw Steve Tshwete – a man whose signature tune was a call on police officers to treat criminals as a bulldog treats a bone – appointed as Minister of Safety and Security in 1999.

Under Tshwete and Jackie Selebi, when he became National Commissioner of the SA Police Service, the language and thinking of police strategists became more aggressive. Whereas the first five years of democracy had seen thinking about policing dominated by a conviction that boots-and-all policing was precisely the wrong thing for the country, the new thinking emphasised cordon-and-search operations in which whole city blocks were closed down, doors were kicked in and anyone suspicious was taken in for questioning. Whereas almost every utterance of the previous minister, Sydney Mufamadi, involved the insistence that the police was only one player among many, and

31

that social transformation was a precondition for improved safety, Tshwete and Selebi presented themselves as men convinced that they sat at the helm of an organisation on the cusp of making inroads into criminality, if it was not actually doing so already. Police transformation was no longer seen as a precondition for success in the fight against crime. The police were ready, willing and able. The new rallying cry, one I heard over and over again, was, 'We're rough and tough and we take no shit.'

This new, much more combative attitude was reflected also in a raft of new legislation pushed through parliament and then defended in the Constitutional Court. This included new bail laws, reversing the earlier changes, and making it significantly harder for arrestees accused of serious crimes to get bail. New sentencing legislation increased dramatically the length of time those convicted of serious criminality would spend in jail, and made South Africa's response to crime more punitive than any in the democratic world. Behind the scenes, Tshwete led a hard-fought campaign to resist the tightening of the rules governing the circumstances under which police officers could shoot fleeing suspects. In the end, his efforts merely delayed promulgation for the best part of five years. They did, however, send a symbolic message to the organisation. It was at the level of resources, though, that the most significant changes took place. Here, rapidly growing police budgets now allowed police numbers, which had shrunk to under 120 000, to begin to grow again. Today the Police Service employs over 160 000 people, and cops are being recruited and trained at the rate of 10 000 a year.

By any standards, these changes in attitude and policy

represented a dramatic turnaround in the fortunes of our law enforcement agencies and, by extension, of the whole idea of law enforcement. But these changes were only part of the story. The other part was a growing sensitivity and defensiveness in government's pronouncements on crime, with both the President and the National Commissioner insisting that perceptions about declining public safety are being driven by fears that are refuted by police crime statistics. This sensitivity, which has sometimes verged on the paranoiac, has skewed public debate about crime and policing, and has left unasked and unanswered important questions about the nature of the crime wave we've lived through and the effectiveness of the state's response.

However awkward, it is this task and these questions – what is the nature of South Africa's crime problem and how effectively has it been addressed? – that this book addresses itself to.

The argument I will make is in four parts. The first is that what makes South Africa's crime problem unique is not so much the volume of crime as its extraordinary violence, with interpersonal violence and the exponential growth in robbery the principal manifestations of this. The second is that our addiction to violence is only partly explained by our history and by our current socio-economic profile. The the rest of the explanation lies in the way in which violence and criminality have themselves come to shape the context within which young men make decisions about how to behave. The third argument is that our crime problem cannot be solved, or even significantly reduced, using current police strategies which focus on preventing crime from happening, and that far more attention needs to be paid to building our capacity to identify, prosecute and incarcerate criminals. The fourth is that moral regeneration cannot be achieved through the lectures of teachers and churches, but demands the rethinking of the process of institution-building right across society, and requires as a precondition a criminal justice system that comes down like a ton of bricks on people who commit violent crimes.

These are potentially controversial claims, and the rest of the book is devoted to proving them.

CHAPTER TWO

THE CRIME CAPITAL OF THE WORLD?

I wrote the first draft of this paragraph on Friday, 8 December 2006. On that day, the front page of *The Star*, my local daily, was packed with stories about crime. The main story recorded the murder of the son of one of the country's leading journalists. The 31-year-old had been found burned to death in the boot of his car hours after phoning his wife to tell her he was being followed by two cars with no license plates that were trying to box him in. The dead man's father told journalists that his only hope was that his son's killers 'killed him before the fire'. Such are the straws a grieving father will clutch. A few weeks later, the dead man's wife was on trial for allegedly plotting the murder.

Below the main story were reports of two other grisly crimes. One was the gang rape of a French tourist walking with her boyfriend near the paddling pools of Durban's beach front. The second was the murder of his wife by a man who subsequently shot himself. It seemed the dead man had had it in for the emergency services because, before he put the gun in his mouth, he shot and wounded a fireman, a paramedic, a security guard and a policeman.

Or so it was reported on 8 December. The following week, it emerged that no police officers had, in fact, been shot at, and that it was late-arriving cops themselves who'd shot at the paramedics, foolish enough to arrive on the scene first and mistaken for criminals by the officers.

In yet another story, at the foot of the page, a court reporter told of the dismissal of murder charges laid against a young woman who, it had been alleged, had helped her husband murder his parents 14 months earlier. The husband and his sister remained on trial.

One sheet of newsprint, then, with four cases of serious violence – the gang rape of a tourist and three murders, one of which also involved a suicide and, perhaps, as many as four attempted murders. For those worried that mere anarchy had been loosed upon the world, the final story on the page, a five-sentence report-let, offered some reassurance: the chiefs of all six metropolitan police forces had issued a statement expressing their belief that the National Commissioner of the SA Police Service, a man whose friendship with an accused murderer and suspected drug smuggler was then under the microscope, would be vindicated in the fullness of time.

Even by Johannesburg's grim standards, the front-page stories that Friday were an unusually gruesome lot. But, in a country in which 50 people are murdered every day, the staggering truth is that this catalogue included only about 4% of the people murdered in the 24 hours before the paper went to print. Some of the remaining murders were reported in the rest of the paper. The others, too common, too banal to spare the requisite column inches, were passed over in silence, news only to the people left behind.

*

Fifty murders a day sounds like a lot. And it is. But it is not a particularly fruitful way of thinking about our crime problems. To see why, consider that about ten years ago the same statement would have been true of the United States which also had over 18 000 murders a year, or 50 every day. Similarly, the figures released by the authorities in the People's Republic of China imply something like 27 000 murders a year, or nearly 75 murders a day.

Whatever the immediacy and rawness of its appeal, the obvious problem with a murders-per-day statistic, as with all crime-time calculations, is that it neglects population numbers. America may have had 50 murders a day in the late 1990s, but it also has seven times more people than we do. Nor is it a surprise that China, with a population 30 times larger than ours, would have more murders a year than South Africa. This is why crime statistics are better expressed in per capita terms − as murders per 1 000 or 100 000 people − if comparisons between jurisdictions or countries are contemplated.

Still, there is something about the absolute numbers that makes them more tangible, more blunt, than the comparatively detoxified per capita figures. Fifty murder victims a day is about a busload of people. The 19 000 people murdered a year would be regarded as a big crowd at any of our cricket or soccer stadiums. And 220 000 deaths − the number of murders in the past ten years in South Africa − is four times larger than the death toll over a similar period of Americans in the Vietnam War, an experience that haunts that country's imagination to this day.

Add to the 19 000 murders the half-million or so cases of assault, serious assault and attempted murder recorded by the police every year, the roughly 200 000 robberies and aggravated robberies, and the 55 000 rapes, to say nothing of the 300 000 burglaries and 85 000 stolen cars and, before we even think about the ocean of crimes that go unreported or unrecorded, it is clear that a substantial portion of South Africans are victims of at least one serious crime every year.

It is almost no exaggeration to describe ourselves as a country at war with itself.

★

No-one who is reading this book needs me to tell him that crime is one of South Africa's most important challenges. Some might say that poverty, unemployment or HIV/AIDS are at least as important but, apart from the occasional publicist or politician, there are no South Africans who even claim to think that our crime rates are in hailing distance of the acceptable. Most of us believe, in fact, that our crime rate is so exceptional as to make our country the 'crime capital of the world'. Given the patchiness of available data and the insurmountable problems besetting any attempt to use police statistics to compare crime in different countries, however, this is a designation whose proof or refutation would be the basis of a good career for an academic criminologist.

One of the biggest problems that our aspirant comparative criminologist would face is that societies define crime differently. In some, it is a crime to insult the president. In others it is legal for a man to beat his wife or worse; in Jordan, generally among the most benign of the Arab states in the treatment of its women, a man may kill an unfaithful wife with legal impunity. Some acts are criminalised in theocracies – idolatry or adultery or homosexuality – but raise barely an eyebrow in secular democracies. Cross-country comparisons of criminality, then, require confining the discussion to specific crimes. But even here there are difficulties. Want to compare countries' aggravated robbery rates? Good luck finding a common definition of 'aggravated'. The same is true of the various species of non-lethal violence – 'assault', 'serious assault' and their near cousin 'attempted murder'. Then there are more narrowly defined crimes that are captured in few countries' official statistics – hijacking, for example. The net result is that police statistics about most crimes are singularly ill-suited for comparative purposes.

If the lack of common definitions is one problem, it pales into insignificance against the variability of reporting and recording practices.

It is simply not true that all victims of crime are everywhere equally likely to report the matter to the police. Are people mugged in Lagos as likely to go to the police as New Yorkers? Will a woman raped by a relative in Saudi Arabia be as likely to call the authorities as one in Sweden? Will a resident of one of Rio's *favellas* report a burglary as conscientiously as a suburbanite in the United Kingdom? In each case the answer is clear: she will not.

There are a lot of reasons why people in different countries – and even in different areas in the same country – are more or less willing to report crimes to their respective police services. Some of these revolve around the likely consequences of reporting the matter. Are the Nigerian police as likely to investigate a mugging as their colleagues in New York? Will the Saudi woman raped by her uncle receive a sympathetic hearing or, given the extraordinary patriarchy of that society, will she expose herself to shame and further trauma? Besides, in some countries – Saudi Arabia included – crimes like these are often dealt with through vendettas rather than formal, records-generating legal systems. And what if burglary victims, by way of another example, generally report their victimisation to the police only if they are insured? How would that affect comparative reporting rates? In much of the third world the decision to go to the police is not helped by the rampant corruption of law enforcement agencies which often act more like uniformed extortion rackets than the bobbies on the beat one might expect to find on the streets of London.

The variability of definition and reporting rates across countries already means that police statistics are hopelessly compromised and cannot be used for cross-country comparisons. The final straw, though, is the variability in the rigour with which different police agencies record the crimes that come to their attention. One issue here is access: to whom, precisely, does one report a crime in the depths of the Congo? Another is the efficiency and transparency of the police bureaucracy. Even if one does report a mugging in Lagos, is the case going to be recorded on any administrative system worthy of the name? Are the figures going to be transmitted up the organisation? Are they going to be accurately collated and then made publicly available? Honestly?

Perhaps all this explains why a compilation of statistics by Interpol arrived at the conclusion that the country in the world with the lowest per capita homicide rate in 2000 was … Pakistan. If this were true, the warlords who run the tribal areas on the border of Afghanistan do not appear to deserve their fearsome reputation. These problems may also go some way towards explaining why the only official murder figure for Nigeria I have ever seen is 20 years old. And why it implies that Nigerians face less risk of being murdered than Australians or Swedes. Perhaps they also account for why, in the midst of at least three civil wars, the Sudanese government was pleased to report a murder rate of three victims per million people in the mid-1990s, a figure that made residents of that benighted country about as safe as the Japanese.

Despite these problems, there are still good reasons for comparing countries' crime rates. It may be true that these comparisons are undermined by the quality of available data, and that they create a sniff of doubt about our designation as the crime capital of the world. But, even with this qualification, those data we do have show that South Africa has absolutely nothing to be proud of.

*

In countries in Western Europe, murder rates average less than two cases per 100 000 people. The same is true of New Zealand, Australia and Canada. In Japan, the figure is less than 1 per 100 000. In the United States, reputedly the most murderous country in the developed world, about 5 people are murdered every year for every 100 000 residents, down from twice that a decade or so ago. In comparison with these countries, our murder rate in 2006, at 41 victims per 100 000 people, is astonishingly high. It is 8 times higher than America's, 20 times higher than Western Europe's, and a staggering 80 times higher than Japan's.

On the plus side, comparing our figures with those in some countries in the developing world can result in less horrifying differences, even if this must rely on more suspect data.

In Colombia various reports put the murder rate at somewhere between 60 and 210 per 100 000. So, in comparison with a country whose major export is cocaine and which has two ongoing civil wars, our murder rate doesn't look all that bad. Venezuelans, Guatemalans, Salvadorians and, according to some estimates, even Brazilians, may have murder rates that may be as high as the mid-30s per 100 000. Here data quality is an issue though, because the highest estimates come from the World Health Organisation which uses a statistical sampling technique to estimate the causes of deaths in countries across the world. In some cases, the samples they use are tiny, and extrapolating from them is very tricky. At the other end of the South American spectrum, however, Chile and Argentina have murder rates comparable to those of the United States, or about one eighth of ours.

In Eastern Europe, a continent in transition, murder rates range from the low single digits per 100 000 in Poland to about 10 in countries like Latvia and Lithuania, and a little more than 20 in Russia.

In the giants of Asia – China and India – reported murder rates are between 3 and 6 per 100 000, though here some scepticism about the figures' reliability may be warranted. About Africa's murder rates, almost nothing reliable is known: Swaziland's is somewhere between 15 and 88 per 100 000, depending on the source; Nigeria, home of a quarter of sub-Saharan Africa's population, hasn't provided a figure to Interpol or the United Nations in two decades, but the World Health Organisation estimates the figure to be in the low 20s per 100 000. It is also not clear what one should make of Interpol reports that in 2000 the Ivory Coast had a murder rate of about 5 per 100 000 given that the World Health Organisation put the number at closer to 30 in 2002.

The data are patchy, then, and the difficulties mean that it is not possible to state conclusively that there are literally no countries in the world in which murder rates are higher than ours. As a result, those with a yen to do so, have ample grounds for expressing doubts about the veracity of this claim. But to go no further than articulate this doubt is disingenuous, for the truth is that our per capita murder rate is in the very, very top bracket, one it shares with broken countries like Sierra Leone. More to the point, every single country in the world that has even remotely decent stats has a murder rate lower than ours. Usually, much, much, much lower.

We may not, therefore, be able to say definitively that there is literally no country with a higher murder rate than ours, but nor is there any evidence to suggest that murder rates here are anything but highly abnormal.

*

A response sometimes offered in the face of these statistics is to point out that there are areas in even the richest countries in the world in which murder rates are higher than ours. There are cities in the United States, for instance, where the risk of being murdered is actually greater than in

South Africa: in Washington DC and New Orleans, for instance, the per capita murder rate is in the range of 40 to 50 per 100 000, a little higher than our national average.

Some people find this kind of thing comforting, so much so that a few years ago, Business Against Crime ran radio adverts suggesting that because murder rates in these cities were higher than ours, we were not, in fact, the crime capital of the world. It is debatable, however, whether there is that much comfort to be drawn from the fact that there are pockets of extremely high levels of violence in the United States. One reason is that national averages are just that – averages. It is a mathematical certainty that in every country there are areas with rates of crime higher than the average and areas with rates that are lower. If the most murderous places in America have homicide rates greater than our national average, precisely the same thing is true of the most murderous places in South Africa. Only in our case, the murder rate in the most violent police precincts – some of them small towns like Stanford and Rhodes – ranges well into the 100s per 100 000, as much as 6 times higher than in America's most violent cities.

There is another reason to question whether the high levels of violence in Washington DC should be any consolation to South Africans: what lesson, precisely, are we to draw from the fact that there are areas in the United States where the authorities, with all America's resources and know-how available to them, have been unable to ensure levels of safety and security that are any better than those in Pretoria or Johannesburg? One lesson might be that our law enforcement agencies and our government departments and our social conditions are no worse than theirs. The alternative is that, even under the best of all possible circumstances, it is far from easy to reduce violence in places where it has become entrenched.

★

The net result of all the statistical problems – inconsistent definitions of crime, under-reporting, under-recording and sheer dishonesty – mean that police statistics cannot tell us whether South Africa really is the crime capital of the world. Fortunately, there is another tool that seeks to overcome some of these deficiencies. This is the victimisation survey, a research tool that provides crime data by asking representative samples of the residents of cities or countries about their experience of criminality over the preceding year.

The great benefit of victimisation surveys is that they ask people directly about crime and, in this way, allow researchers in different countries to use common definitions. As importantly, they eliminate the data gaps that arise from inconsistencies in reporting rates, inaccuracies of data-collection methodologies, and the dishonesty of police agencies and their political masters. There are, however, important problems with victimisation surveys. They are expensive, for one, and, as a result, data at a national level are available for only a few countries outside the developed world. A second problem is that no-one has found a method for surveying murder victims, so this is not a crime that can be measured in this way. A final problem relates to interpretation: it may be possible that people asked the same question in two different places or at two different times will understand the nature of the enquiry differently. This may help explain the unexpected finding that respondents in countries like Finland, Austria and New Zealand report being the victims of sexual assault about ten times more frequently than respondents in South Africa.

These qualifications affect how we interpret the results of victimisation surveys when we compare them across countries. But there remain lessons that can be drawn from these studies, some of them surprising. A victimisation survey done in South Africa in 2003, for instance, found that just less than 23% of all South Africans were the victims of a crime in the previous year. That put us as low as 11th on the list of 25 countries in which these surveys have been run. The surprise is that the top five positions were taken by Australia (30%), New Zealand (29%), England (26%), Holland (25%) and Sweden (25%).

Now, it is quite possible that people have different standards about what they consider an assault or a sexual assault and that this has skewed the results. It is also possible that people from different cultures are not equally happy to tell strangers about violence done to them, especially if it was done by friends or intimates. But matters are different in relation to property crime. These results should be reliable because people who are burgled or mugged or who have their pockets picked in Brisbane shouldn't be blessed with better memories, or a greater willingness to report the event to a researcher, than are victims of similar crimes in Benoni. It is significant, then, that in relation to non-violent property crime, South Africans report being victims at roughly the same rate as people in New Zealand, Australia, England, Italy, Canada and the USA, all of whom report property crime rates of between 10% and 14%.

Before the dancing in the street breaks out, there is an

46

important qualification to add. This is that the mid-table ranking that emerges from cross-country comparisons based on victimisation data depends greatly on whether it is true in other countries, as it is here, that people between the ages of 12 and 22 are victimised at roughly twice the adult rate. The reason this is important is that the figures I cited above rely on surveys which ask questions only of people older than 18. This is true of surveys in other countries, too. Much depends, therefore, on whether young people in all countries are just as prone to becoming victims as they are in South Africa. If they are not, then our national surveys underestimate the true crime rate and do so in ways that may not be true of surveys in other countries.

Even if this factor makes no difference, one of the results that does emerge from existing surveys is tragically predictable: in comparison with the countries that have conducted victimisation surveys, the rate at which South Africans are robbed is at least three times higher than the average.

Robbery, which is by definition a crime of violence because it amounts to a theft committed by someone who uses violence or threatens to do so, occurs more frequently here than it does in even the most crime-prone countries of Latin America. This is especially true of armed robbery where a survey conducted in Johannesburg in 2000 found that nearly 80% of robbery victims reported that their attacker had used a gun. I know of no survey that has ever found a higher proportion of robbery victims having to face armed assailants anywhere else in the world. In most countries, including in the developed world, robbers are armed in fewer than one incident in five.

*

47

The bottom line, then, is that Chris Stone, the Harvard criminologist, has it right when he says that 'the distinctive feature of crime in South Africa is not its volume but its violence.' Our murder rate is exceptionally high by world standards. So, too, is the robbery rate, especially the armed variety. Property crime that involves no violence, by contrast, is no worse than in other countries. As a nation, in other words, our problem is an unhealthy addiction to violence, not to law-breaking in general. Before looking at the reasons for this and what we need to do to break the addiction, we need to ask a highly charged question: is it getting worse?

CHAPTER THREE

IS IT GETTING WORSE?
THE FACTS (AND POLITICS) OF FEAR

Here's an under-appreciated fact about murder in South Africa: the 53 homicides recorded every day in 2006 actually represented a significant improvement in public safety; a decade ago, the daily toll was nearly 75 people. Since its peak in the mid-1990s, the number of murders recorded every year has fallen by 30% from nearly 27 000 to about 19 000.

The decline in murder rates is not an insignificant achievement and it raises an important question: if murder rates have been coming down, and for some time, why do South Africans think that crime is getting worse? This is a key problem for a government that sincerely believes that the facts about crime belie South Africans' ingrained despair over it. If murder has been going down, it insists, and going down relatively rapidly, why do so many people think that government lacks the will or ability to reduce crime? Sometimes the answer government supplies to this question is that too many opinion-formers are white and that their racist fears underpin their gloomy perceptions. There is another answer to this question, though. This is that what has happened with murder rates is only half of the post-apartheid crime story. The other half is the rapid rise in robbery.

★

Ten years ago, in 1995/96, the South African Police Service recorded about 27 000 murders. It is the highest number of victims in a single year on record. In the same year, it recorded about 77 000 armed robberies and 46 000 robberies committed by offenders who had no firearms. In sum, there were about five times more robberies recorded by the police than murders. Eleven years later, the number of murders had fallen to 19 200, but the number of recorded robberies had risen dramatically – to 195 000, of which 126 000 were armed robberies. By that point, the number of robberies outnumbered murders by more than ten to one, twice the ratio of a decade earlier. Dramatic as this change in the shape of South African crime appears, it may actually understate matters because the 198 000 robberies recorded in 2006/07 was 14% lower than the 230 000 of three years before, a decline that seems implausibly large and to which I will return.

★

There are many people in government and elsewhere who profess a belief that the rise in robberies recorded by the police over the past decade is little more than a statistical illusion, one that flows from a presumed increase in the willingness of people to report crimes to the authorities. This, so the argument goes, is one of the consequences of the transformation of a society in which the majority once saw no reason to report crimes to a police force that was dedicated to upholding apartheid rather than chasing down a township's muggers. After 1994, and the inculcation of an ethos of community service into the SAPS, they argue, many more victims have been willing to come forward. The police, for their part, have also become much more aware of the need to help the community and are now recording incidents more conscientiously. It is these processes, so the argument goes, not an increase in the actual number of crimes committed, that explains the rise in reported robbery.

For those who buy it, this argument seems to be confirmed by the decline in murder: if murder, by far the best-reported and best-recorded crime is coming down, surely that means that there is less to the rise in other forms of criminality than meets the eye?

To give government its due, increased reporting may actually be part of the reason robbery rates rose after 1994. But there is no reason why an increased willingness to report crime could not occur while crime rates were actually rising. In fact, you might think that this was a perfectly plausible coincidence since increased criminality may make people more anxious to help the police.

A more significant problem for those who think that increased reporting explains the rise in robbery is that there is actually evidence that the opposite occurred. This comes from a national victimisation survey completed in 2003 which found that only 29% of people who said they'd been robbed in the previous 12 months confirmed that they had reported the incident to the police. This was significantly lower than the 41% of robbery victims who had given the same answer to the question five years earlier, a trend that is exactly the opposite of what believers in the continuously improving legitimacy of the police would have expected.

Now, I have my doubts about these two surveys and their

representativity, making it hard to be sure that reporting rates actually fell as far or as fast as these results suggest. Still, it would be disingenuous not to note that the 2003 survey did not find that reporting rates had increased, putting a big question mark against any claim that this explains the rise in robbery. Nor is there any reason to think that they should have increased from the 41% recorded in 1998 since even in North America, only about 50% of robbery victims report the crime to the authorities. In the developing world, the proportion is closer to 30%. It may be that our cops enjoy more enthusiastic public support than most in the developing world because they are less corrupt and more professional than their colleagues in most of these countries, but their legitimacy and accessibility don't approach those of the developed north. There is, therefore, no reason to think that reporting rates here are ever going to be as high as they are there.

The best that can be said, then, is that even if reporting rates did rise after 1994, they seem to have stopped doing so sometime in the late 1990s and may well have fallen back after that. If that is what happened, the rise in the number of robberies recorded by the police after 1998 understates what was actually happening, and doubts must arise about the recently recorded fall in robbery.

Apart from all of this, there are other reasons to question the claim that the rise in robbery over the past decade is a statistical illusion. One issue is that it is hard to explain why increased police accessibility and legitimacy would have encouraged robbery victims to report the crime, but would not have led rape survivors to do the same. This is a crime that everyone believes to be under-reported, yet the 2006 figure is barely 2% higher than that of 1996. Another problem for the reporting-rates-did-it school of thought comes from that tightly calibrated scientific measuring device known by its technical name, 'common sense': there is simply too much anecdotal evidence that suggests a dramatic rise in robbery rates over the past decade for anyone, apart from the wilfully deluded, seriously to question the conclusion.

All of which raises an intriguing question: if robbery rates were rocketing through the roof, why is it that murder was falling? The short answer is that only a small proportion of murders are committed in the course of a robbery. Most are the result of what analysts in South Africa have taken to calling 'interpersonal violence', a category of crime that covers everything from domestic violence to road rage, from a barroom brawl to a violent dispute between an employee and his boss. The police, through the person of their Minister, take the official view that as many as 80% of murders fall in this category. This, I have argued elsewhere, is almost certainly wrong and is based on a mistaken reading of police data. Nevertheless, it is not implausible to think that something like half of all murders are committed by people who know their victims. That being so, there is no reason to expect that a dramatic rise in robbery (and even a dramatic rise in robbery-murders) must inevitably lead to a rise in the total number of murders recorded. If levels of lethal interpersonal violence were falling while robbery and robbery-murder rates were rising, it is quite possible that the decline of one would conceal the rise in the other. Just as importantly for a ten-year time horizon, the mid-1990s was a period in which political violence in KwaZulu-Natal and

Gauteng was still relatively commonplace. As this category of violence worked itself out of the system, murder rates might have fallen even if robbery-murders doubled or tripled.

Like the statistician's proverbial bikini, what the fall in murder obscures about the crime wave of the 1990s may be more interesting than what it reveals.

★

If we reject the idea that increased reporting explains the rise in robbery and accept that people are right to think that the risk of robbery has grown exponentially, we have to try to explain why it might have happened. Inevitably, there are a range of factors at work. Some of these have to do with the structure of our society, its basic character. One of these is our rapid urbanisation.

It is common cause among criminologists that people who live in cities are much more likely to be robbed than are people who live in the rural hinterland. This is not because the peasants and farmers and small-townsmen who live in the countryside are better, more moral people than those of us who live in the city. It is because the anonymity that flows from living in the mass society of modern cities means that it is far, far easier for city-dwelling robbers to get away with their crimes. In small communities, by contrast, people tend to know each other better, and the chances that a knife-wielding mugger will be caught are much higher. Besides, it is psychologically harder to threaten the life of someone you know or with whom you share certain social bonds, making robberies in rural areas less common.

If the anonymity of our cities facilitates robbery, then the rapid urbanisation that has taken place in the past two or three decades, and which accelerated after the death of apartheid, will have led to an increase in robbery rates all by itself. Add to that our less-than-impressive performance in creating jobs for the cities' new arrivals, and you have the beginnings of a theory both about the rise in robbery and about its spatial concentration in urban areas.

Other reasons why robbery rates increased are more banal. It is a fact of modern life, for instance, that the introduction of high-value, easily transported consumer goods has often been followed by an increase in crime. Burglary rates rose in the United Kingdom when television was introduced, and did so again when video machines came onto the market. The timing of the introduction of these items into the South African market cannot explain the rise in robbery in the 1990s. Cellphones are another matter, and their penetration into our lives coincides closely with an increased risk of mugging.

But neither urbanisation nor cellphones feels anything like a full account of why robbery exploded after 1994. This, I think, had more to do with the depth to which violence has penetrated our national psyche. This is a subject which deserves, and will receive, more discussion later. For the moment let us just note that one of the challenges of combating criminality is the powerful self-reinforcing processes that are at play, forces that have allowed a culture of crime to take hold in much the same way as a particular brand can take hold of the imagination of the clothes-buying public.

★

Let us put aside for the moment all the usual factors people cite when they talk about the causes of South Africa's crime problem. Let us forget for a minute about the links between crime and unemployment or demographic changes, or between violence and our history of oppression and cruelty. Let us, instead, put ourselves in the shoes of someone who falls into that category of people that South African criminologists have taken to calling 'at risk', the group who may come into 'conflict with the law'. Let us ask what the consequences are of the fact that they live in a high-crime environment. How might that context shape their choices?

One way to think about this is to assume that there is a good chance that, in the right circumstances, almost anyone would commit a crime, even a violent one. Perhaps there is a small, saintly minority who would never contemplate committing a crime, but it is more likely that, in the right context, almost anyone would. But what is it in the context that decides things? What are the circumstances that determine whether you or I or anyone else commits crime?

Naturally, socio-economic issues are among the most important. But there is another that might be as important. This is the behaviour of other people, the decisions they make about committing a crime or choosing not to.

This idea occurred to me when I was stuck in heavy traffic on a highway in Johannesburg. I was virtually stationary in the left-hand lane, while the emergency lane to my left was open. It stayed that way for a while, and hundreds of people behind and in front of me disregarded the advantage each of us could gain if we just moved into the wide-open spaces that were, admittedly, reserved for ambulances, police cars and tow-trucks. None of us moved because we all knew that to do so was wrong: that lane is for emergencies, and, besides, it's not fair on everyone else who is playing by the rules.

And then it happened. One driver – of a taxi, inevitably – shifted onto the hard shoulder and raced past. And then, the ice broken, another driver did it. And then another and another. Soon the extra lane was filling up and, however strictly I might have felt about not using that lane ten minutes earlier, when the first housewife drove by I thought, 'What the hell?' And off I went.

The essence of this story is not that once lane-abuse took hold, it changed my values. It is that these kinds of values are never absolutes. They are conditional, and one of the things that they are conditional on is what everyone else is doing: we will join in activities we know to be wrong if enough people are doing them. My move into the emergency lane wasn't because my values had changed. What had changed was the context in which I was making my choices: at some point, enough people were involved for me to think that driving in the emergency lane was something 'everyone' does. And if 'everyone' does it, why shouldn't I?

I think the same process is at work in a crime wave. I may want to believe that I could never, ever rob someone at knife point, but is it true? What if I needed the money and, as importantly, I lived on a street where a sizeable chunk of men my age made their income this way? Wouldn't that change my behaviour? I'm pretty sure I would never delude myself into thinking that robbery was morally OK. But I might very well come to think that one more robber on the street – me – wasn't going to make a whole lot of difference to the world.

If something like this occurred in South Africa in the 1990s, then, as the number of people involved in robbery climbed, that process by itself, rather than any deterioration of material conditions, might have pulled more and more people into crime. It may be no exaggeration to say that the robbery meltdown we've seen over the past ten years is not the result of some sudden shift in economic or social conditions or by the penetration of cellphones into the market, but by the more insidious process of social diffusion. This has turned an already high level of violence – the origins of which I will try to explain later – into a runaway chain-reaction of criminality, one that has continued to feed off its own energy ever since.

I will return to this idea, and what it means for law enforcement, later.

★

If it is true that for ten years the explosion in robbery rates has fed off its own momentum, what should we make of the dramatic fall in the number of robberies recorded by the police after 2003? These fell by nearly 16% over two years, from nearly 230 000 in 2003/04 to under 195 000 in 2005/06 and 198 000 the following year. Was this the much-vaunted turnaround, a sign that the vicious cycle had been damp-ened down and that improved policing now meant that the meltdown was cooling off? That, certainly, is the view of the National Commissioner of the SAPS.

Anyone who wanted to show that the decline in recorded robbery reflected what was really going on, and looked for reasons to explain it, could choose any of a number of plausible candidates as catalyst-in-chief. These include the increasing numbers of police officers on the street or, considerably less credibly, the spread of sector policing methodologies to more and more police stations. For those with an eye on root causes, the rising levels of employment and the rapid expansion of the social safety net might offer themselves as reasons for the decline. An alternative explanation, though a debatable one, might focus on the impact, delayed though it may have been, of the minimum sentences legislation and increased average sentences. All of these factors, together with the social and political stability that democracy has brought as well as the uncounted, unrecognised initiatives by churches and NGOs and community groups and ordinary citizens, might have disrupted the processes which for a decade had led to the explosion in robbery rates. There is, after all, no reason to think that we are condemned to an ever-worsening crime problem.

But, with the best will in the world, it's hard to believe that there were 14% fewer robberies in 2006 than there were in 2003. A decline of this size is simply too large to credit, and it is hard not to believe that something else might be going on. And here, two possibilities present themselves. The first is a decline in the willingness of people to report robberies to the police. The second is that the police are choosing to record fewer crimes.

One reason reporting rates might have dropped suddenly in 2005 could be the changes made to the rules governing when a police station may open a case after a victim has been relieved of his cellphone, changes that were instituted at almost exactly the time that robbery statistics peaked. These rules now require that a cellphone be blocked by the service provider, and that a victim of robbery provide proof of blacklisting before a case can be opened. Now, in general, blacklisting is a very, very good thing because it has the potential to disrupt the market for stolen cellphones and also helps to curb insurance fraud, so these changes may well have been justified. At the same time, the increase in the annoyance factor may have discouraged the reporting of crime because people robbed of an uninsured, pay-as-you-go cellphone seldom care if the thing is blacklisted. Why would they? After all, some industry experts think that even before these changes were introduced only a tenth of the half-million-plus phones stolen were reported to the police.

The second candidate for explaining the size of the apparent decline in robbery is more troubling. This is that the increased use being made of a station's crime statistics to assess its performance may be discouraging cops from entering reported crimes onto their systems. This was something I saw myself in 2003 when a senior officer in Johannesburg told me she regretted the arrest her officers had made of a mugger because 'robbery is a serious crime. Now we will have to open a docket and our crime stats are going to look bad.' Even before that experience, a senior officer responsible for compiling crime statistics for the Police Service told me of a station commissioner who'd been caught running two systems to record crime. One was run on a stand-alone PC which kicked out a case number the victim could use for insurance purposes, but whose data would never be entered on the national database.

If these two examples pre-date the aggressive roll-out of quantitative metrics of performance now being deployed to measure stations' performance, how much greater must the incentive now be to cook the books?

It is, in other words, no surprise to me that the statistics started to fall at precisely the moment that senior police management started holding station commissioners' feet to the fire in an effort to hit annual targets for a 7% reduction in violent crime. Police management seems sometimes to have forgotten that it is usually easier for stations to reduce the statistics than it is for them to reduce the crime. Local cops know, after all, that their figures are entirely unauditable; they are their own master set.

*

The rise in robbery over the past ten years is not 'just' a raw increase in the number of crimes committed, something that the police and government can treat as a technical challenge for its law enforcement agencies. While being all of that, the crime wave has also metastasised into one of the most significant and poisonous political developments of the past decade, largely because ours is a deeply divided nation.

White South Africans tend to be richer than their black compatriots. They have better education, better jobs, better houses. They live in suburbs with better roads and water and street lighting. They are less dependent on deadly public transport and shambolic public health services. They are also, as far as I can tell, much less likely to be murdered.

The best data we have on the racial profile of murder victims comes from the Medical Research Council which tracks patterns of non-natural death – of which motor accidents and homicides are by far the most common – by keeping tabs on corpses arriving at the country's morgues. Since 2002, for reasons that involve frustration at the inaccurate use made of some of the statistics together with a side-order of misplaced political correctness, the MRC has chosen not to provide details on the race of people arriving at our morgues. In 2001, however, when these data were last made available, fewer than 5% of murder victims arriving at our morgues were white. Given that whites make up nearly 10% of the population, this meant that their per capita murder rate was about half the national average. Being white, it turns out, made it significantly less likely that you'd be murdered. Nor were white South Africans the only demographic group to face substantially less risk of murder. The same was true of Indians, of women of all races (who are victims of only about 13% of all homicides) as well as both the very young and the very old.

We don't know everything about who gets murdered in South Africa, but we do know that some people – young black men, especially – face much greater risks than others. Even by the miserable standards of the data we have about the profile of murder victims, though, what we know about the profile of robbery victims is ludicrously bad.

It is generally believed that victims of robbery also tend to be black. This we deduce from the fact that most robberies take place in our urban ghettos, the inner cities and the townships on the periphery of the largest metropolitan areas. But even if only a minority of robbery victims are white, they are much better represented in the population of robbery victims than they are in the population of murder victims. This is a conclusion that emerges from an analysis of the spatial distribution of murder and robbery, which shows that there is proportionately far more robbery in the suburbs than there is murder, and that a suburbanite's risk of being robbed is much closer to the risk faced by people in our urban ghettos. In fact, as early as July 1997, white respondents to a victimisation survey in Johannesburg were as likely as anyone else to report having been robbed or mugged in the previous 12 months.

Robbery, unlike murder, does not discriminate.

Or, to be more accurate, it does discriminate: some robbers actively seek out the rich. And the result has been that the annual number of armed robberies – a category that includes hijacking – recorded at police stations in South Africa's richest suburbs doubled, tripled and, in some cases, quadrupled between 1995 and 2003. There, it shook South Africa's middle classes to their roots.

*

Counter-factual histories are a dubious parlour game, but ask yourself how South Africa's predominantly white middle classes would relate to the new South Africa if the past decade had not seen an explosion of violence around them.

This is a group of people for whom democracy has proven to be enormously beneficial, having brought with it re-entry into the global circuits of commerce and culture and sport. As a group, they have grown richer financially, culturally and in all other meaningful ways. And yet many live lives in the grip of something akin to terror, the principal source of which is the violence that has exploded into their lives.

Were it not for the crime wave, South Africa's white community might have been among the happiest groups of people in the world. There would still have been some difficulties; crime is not the only reason white South Africans give for the malaise they feel. Affirmative action, the declining importance of Afrikaans in public life, inadequate maintenance of the roads and issues in the health and education systems ... there are any number of quibbles, cloaked sometimes by a crocodile-teared concern for the poor, that white South Africans have with the new South Africa. Some of these anxieties draw on racist assumptions about the competence and honesty of democratic governance. They draw also on an abiding, unarticulated sense of disenfranchisement, of being a ruling class deprived of its power. They would, therefore, exist whether the crime wave had happened or not.

But the fear of crime is different from these other concerns. More so than the issues of service delivery, the eruption of predatory crime has been dislocating and traumatic. The experience is terrifying and devastating in its own right, but it is also an unambiguous confirmation of one's powerlessness, of the precariousness of one's existence. And the awareness of powerlessness reinforces the trauma and terror of the act itself. Potholes in the streets and declining educational standards cannot begin to create the kind of vertiginous horror that the experience of violent crime has generated. Had this not happened, it is not far-fetched to imagine that everything that speaks to the mood of white South Africans – from voting patterns and our newspapers' letters pages to the content of President Mbeki's blog – might look very, very different.

If violence is an emotive issue, it is also profoundly political because it goes to the heart of the social contract between a state and its citizenry. High levels of crime inevitably erode confidence in government. This might be offset by government's making progress in other areas, but the fear of vicious, potentially lethal violence must always leave lingering in people's minds a suspicion that the state is somehow deficient, that something about it is rotten. Matters are even more politically challenging when a community experiences a surge of violence of the scale of the explosion in hijackings and robberies beginning in the mid- and late 1990s. It would be no exaggeration to say that for many, the threat felt existential; it was as if their whole social structure was being torn apart. Little wonder that since the late 1990s, white South Africans have insisted that crime is the country's most serious challenge.

Seen from one perspective, there is something selfish and self-regarding in this. Crime, after all, has rent apart the families of black South Africans for generations. It has traumatised and brutalised people who had (and have) no access to private security or insurance policies, people who, until recently, have also had little recourse to the police. It is horribly unjust that it is crime's movement into the suburbs – rather than its already high levels in the townships – that has made violence so significant politically. That, though, is the reality of politics in an unequal society: the problems of the elite always receive more attention than the problems of the marginalised. The result is that, however impressive the decline in lethal interpersonal violence, it is the rising robbery rates and the eruption of violence into the lives of the largely white middle classes that this has brought, that has driven the vexed politics of crime.

And, all too often, government's responses to this have only made things worse.

Among the least effective of its responses to the panic the middle classes feel is the oft-deployed argument that things are worse elsewhere, that the poor have to live with far more violence, and have done for generations. This may be true, but in making it, government demonstrates a counterproductive lack of sympathy, a tone-deafness that verges on denialism. Nor is it especially helpful, in this context, to argue that national murder rates are coming down. Even when this claim is true, it is all but irrelevant to suburbanites living through an unprecedented crime wave. They simply do not believe it. Least helpful of all responses, though, have been the president's ruminations about the way in which racist fears of black people have fuelled the fear of crime.

The thrust of the president's point – that the white community's historical fears of the black majority have transmogrified into fears of crime, and that the force of white fears has been strengthened by conscious and unconscious racism – is almost certainly true. It is also true, I think, that the fear of crime has sometimes become a conveniently 'apolitical' vehicle through which a disenfranchised elite can mourn its loss of power without sounding nostalgic for an unjust past. But there is an equal and opposite truth: crime, and the fear it generates, has helped to sustain the racist fear of black people the president bemoans, and has made the quest for ever-improving levels of domestic and foreign credibility harder to achieve.

Saying that crime has helped keep the embers of nostalgia for apartheid burning may be to overstate matters. But it has made it much, much harder for government to win over its critics, amongst whom the conviction has grown that, apparently in denial about the nature of the problem, government has given up trying to improve their safety.

★

It is hard to overstate how important the post-liberation crime wave has been in shaping attitudes to the new South Africa among the (predominantly white) middle classes. As a result, the answer to the question of whether South African crime is getting worse, like the answers to so many questions, is that it depends a great deal on whom you ask.

Members of the middle classes, especially those whose skin colour means they come from a community that has lived in the security bubble created by apartheid, have good reason to think that crime has worsened. Certainly, their personal experience of it has. Given the power this community has in influencing public opinion, it is little wonder that the national mood on these issues is so dark.

While the pace of deterioration in the townships and urban ghettos may not have been as rapid, the same is probably true of the poor: as robbery rates have surged, they too have become the victims of more and more crime, even as the risk of being murdered has fallen. Here, too, the rise and rise of predatory crime has undercut whatever improvements in the public's sense of safety that may have flowed from improving murder rates and, despite government's repeated attempts to focus on the latter, it is the former that has tended to shape public opinion.

The trouble is that dealing with a surge of predatory crime requires a good deal more than just finding the right rhetorical formulas to manage public fears.

CHAPTER FOUR

WHY A PLAGUE OF ROBBERY IS SO DIFFICULT TO CURE

Six or seven years ago, I was involved in a project with the Banking Council, which sought to bring police and security personnel together to look at how to reduce the number of bank robberies and cash-in-transit heists. Given the continuing problems our banks face, some will conclude that our efforts were fruitless and that I have no business passing myself off as an expert on crime. In fact, much was achieved by the team, some of which persists today in the form of the ongoing cooperation between the banks, the security companies and the police. The reality is, though, that preventing these robberies is obscenely difficult, primarily because the maths are against us.

On any given day, there are something like 1 000 cash-in-transit vehicles on South Africa's roads, transporting hundreds of millions of rands between businesses and their banks, as well as between the banks' various branches, their cash depots and their ATMs. The physical movement of cash in this way generates near-infinite opportunities for gangs either to attack security guards as they leave their clients' premises with bags and boxes filled with cash, or, between stops, as they travel the country's roads. In the face of all these opportunities, the number of cash-in-transit robberies recorded by the police in 2006/7, at fewer than 500, is actually quite small. In fact, there are countries with far more incidents than this: in the United Kingdom over 700 raids of this sort are recorded every year. This is in embarrassing contrast with Germany which had fewer than twenty. In that country, though, the largest security company in the field collapsed when its managers were tried for skimming cash off the top of their payloads.

Back in South Africa, we have something less than two incidents a day. With 1 000-odd vehicles each doing dozens of pick-ups and drop-offs every day, that means that the risk that any particular shipment will be robbed is minuscule, and that there are pretty tight limits on how much it is worth spending to improve security. Especially since much of the risk can be insured, with the costs passed on to the customer. Cold-hearted business it may be, but the bottom line is that what matters most to the banks and security companies is just that – the bottom line.

Besides, even if they spent the earth, there is only so far that security companies can go in securing the money they move. This was a point that was made quite strongly to me when I discussed the issue of the cash vans' security with a retired executive from one of the bigger companies involved in the business. The man, who would not want his name to appear in this book and whom I shall call 'Stefaans', was in his sixties, and his face, cragged and burnt from the years he'd spent on the border with the SADF, spoke of an active life. We met in Sandton City, one of Johannesburg's biggest malls, and a place he'd selected because he wanted to show me how easy it would be to rob security guards. 'Those malls are crawling with my guards,' he'd said on the phone. 'We won't have to wait long to find one. Then you'll see what we're up against.'

As it happens, we didn't find a guard to observe particularly quickly, but the coffee and cakes were good, so the time wasn't wasted. 'There they are,' he said at last. 'Let me show you something.'

Coming down one of the corridors were two men, one walking ahead of the other, both with hands on pistols that were strapped to the body armour on their chests. They were young and strong, and they seemed to be taking their jobs as seriously as would anyone whose profession made him a target for potentially homicidal gangs.

'Look at them, the poor bastards,' Stefaans said. 'They've got a pick-up in the mall and they've got to get to the customer. But they've got no choice about what route to take: they must come in through the same door that everyone else uses and they must follow the same passages. Anyone could ambush them anywhere. Their movements are completely predictable.'

As he spoke, the two men walked into a large clothing store.

'Look at the terrain,' Stefaans continued. 'It's full of people. Any of them could be an attacker. All they need is two people with nine mills to put to the guards' heads. That's all it would take. And, if they're smart, it'll happen so fast that these guys won't even get their guns out: they can't fight back, not with guns to their heads. In any case, in a place like this, the stores definitely don't want our guards defending themselves too aggressively; it's bad for business. So if someone does put a gun to these guys' heads, the bag's definitely gone. They can get anything in there. Fifty grand, maybe. Maybe a hundred. They probably don't even have to kill anyone. And where's the risk to them?

'People think that the CIT problem is about vans getting hit on the highway. It's not. It's in malls like this and in the shopping areas in the CBD and in townships. Everywhere that the guards have to go to fetch the cash. Those environments can't be managed, so the guards are sitting ducks if someone wants to attack them. The element of surprise is always with the attacker. Always.'

'So the challenge is to keep the guards vigilant,' I said. It was a sentence, but I let my voice rise to turn it into a question.

Stefaans just snorted. 'Vigilant?' he said. 'It's not about vigilance. It's about the element of surprise and, unless the attacker is a complete fucking amateur, he's always going to have it. When I was in the military, they taught us that in any contact with the enemy, nothing is more important than the element of surprise. If your enemy's got it, then the only things that are going to keep you alive are superior numbers or superior firepower. Otherwise you're cooked.'

'So what about more numbers? Or heavier weapons? Why not arm these guys better?'

'Because, if you do that, you've got an arms race on your hands. And that's not good for bystanders.' He paused and then asked me a surprising question: 'What do you think is a security guard's job?'

I must have looked at him funny, because he repeated the question. 'I'm serious,' he said. 'What's his job?'

'To protect cash?' I asked, making it clear that I knew I was going to be told I was wrong.

'No,' he said. 'A security guard's job is to become a

statistic. We give him a gun and some training and a bag full of money to look after. His job is to die.'

This seemed nuts to me, as it was intended, so I asked him to explain.

'You can see what it's like. Against anyone with two brain cells to rub together, these guys have almost no chance. So what their job is, is to send a message to anyone who wants to rob them that, sure, they can do it. But only if they are willing to kill. They could get caught or killed. There is a chance of that. But that's a risk they can manage. What they have to accept, though, is that there is a chance they'll have to kill someone. So basically, a guard's job is to send a message: "You can take our money, but only if you're willing to kill someone if you have to."'

I contemplated what Stefaans had said, wondering at the notion that guards were a kind of implicit moral hurdle over which we dared attackers to leap, one that could be erected only because their labour is cheap relative to the other options. 'But there are a lot of people willing to kill,' I said.

'And that, my friend, is why we have so many cash-in-transit robberies. And the more security we throw at the problem, the more violent the robbers will be.'

What he said next could pass as a summary of this book: 'The best thing we can do is try to catch the fuckers afterwards.'

*

My conversation with Stefaans was not the first time that anyone had ever cautioned me that increased security sometimes had the perverse effect of raising the level of violence used to commit a crime. That, after all, is the textbook account for the rise in hijacking: as motor vehicles became increasingly difficult to steal without their keys, thieves had to confront the driver more often. Hijacking, in the language of criminologists, is displaced car theft, and it emerged as we loaded our cars with as much theft-prevention processing power as the Americans used to put a man on the moon.

Another version of this security-begets-violence argument I have heard is more troubling still. It was related to me by a police officer based at the Bramley Police Station in Johannesburg in the late 1990s. I was working at the time on a docket analysis of gun crimes committed there and in neighbouring Alexandra over a three-month period. My work involved reading scores and scores of cases of armed robbery, many of which were carjackings, and a smaller number of murders, attempted murders and pointings of a firearm. At the time, Bramley had one of the biggest carjacking problems in South Africa and, even in the absence of comparative data, I imagine that that made it one of world's most fiery hijacking hot-spots.

Having spent a couple of weeks reading the dockets, I sat down with one of the station's senior cops and pointed out to him that, when I began the work, I had had the preconceived idea that many more carjackings would have involved a shooting. In fact, it was only in a tiny minority of incidents that the victim was injured, killed or even shot at. For the most part the car was taken, and a shaken, but otherwise unharmed driver, was left at the side of the road.

'It's true,' the officer said to me. 'Mostly, these crimes are not violent.'

Having a gun stuck in one's face with the demand that one's car keys be handed over is, I think, most people's idea of violence, so, when the officer said that this was not usually a violent crime, he must have meant that no-one was physically harmed in the incident. 'Things were different a few months ago,' he went on, talking about a period that would have been about 18 months after the last of the cases I had looked at. 'We had a couple of murders then. Two drivers were killed in one week.'

'Why?' I asked. 'What changed?'

'We're not sure,' he replied. 'But we think they were sending us a message. You see, before they killed the two victims, we'd had an incident when Flying Squad units chased some of the hijackers into Alex. They killed two of them. We think maybe the murders were a message: "If you kill us, we'll kill the *haasmanne.*" It was like they were holding a gun to our heads.'

*

The most general way to make the point about the emergence of hijacking in response to the increased sophistication of anti-theft devices is that one effect of any successful crime prevention initiative is that criminals develop new techniques, target new victims, or commit their crimes in new areas. An argument one often hears, in this regard, is that the net effect on crime of boomed-off roads and high-security villages is negligible since, in protecting themselves against crime, residents of these areas simply pass a heightened risk of victimisation on to others.

Stated in its strongest terms, it cannot possibly be true

that every conceivable enhancement in security will fail to improve public safety because all the 'prevented' crime will shift on to other people. Only careful empirical work, of the kind all too seldom done in South Africa, can determine the precise effects of any particular strategy. What I do accept, though, is that at least some crime will be displaced, rather than completely prevented, whenever crime prevention activities work. It is even possible that some kinds of displacement make people less safe, as was the case when car-theft syndicates turned to hijacking as theft-prevention technology improved. Another example of this phenomenon may be the impact of tracker devices, which came onto the market in the late 1990s.

By making both car theft and hijacking more risky, tracking technology seems to have helped to reduce car theft and hijacking by 20% between 1998 and 2005. Conceivably, this could have led to a decline in crime overall, as appears to have been the case in the United States. In South Africa, however, the answer to the question, 'What does a car thief do when he is not stealing cars?' appears to be that he turns to other forms of crime. So the penetration of tracker technology into the market may have increased the risk of driveway robberies (where a driver is relieved of everything of value except his car), home robberies, restaurant robberies and even simple mugging. Unfortunately, because some of these crimes net the perpetrator less than the average car theft or hijacking, it may be that when our disgruntled would-be car thief turns to robbery, he has to commit more crimes to generate the same income. Thus, tracker devices may have lowered car crime, but may also have pushed up other forms of criminality.

The logic of displacement is also part of the explanation for why cash-in-transit heists have become a feature of the criminal landscape. These emerged as new technology and security systems made banks both harder targets as well as less lucrative ones. Later, as security companies invested in more secure vehicles and improved the vetting of their own staff, some of the criminal energy expended on cash-in-transit heists was devoted to attacking the stores and super-markets that generate the cash in the first place.

The fact that successful crime prevention initiatives often have the unintended effect of displacing crime creates a potentially paralysing moral dilemma: is it right, we are asked, for one person to increase his own protection against crime in a manner that exposes others to increased risk?

There are two kinds of responses to this question. The first response is that, if it is true that criminals respond to some forms of policing and security by ratcheting up the amount of violence they use, the reverse will also be the case; in response to some forms of security and policing, they might be encouraged to rely less on violence. If, for instance, we could engineer an increased risk of detection and prosecution for violent criminals, it may be that non-violent approaches will become that much more attractive. This was the premise of a highly respected, profoundly influential strategy used in Boston to combat gangsterism which focused a dispropor-tionately large share of law enforcement attention on gangs whose members used violence, while treating the others relatively leniently. The approach takes for granted that levels of violence in a society are co-managed: government cannot simply declare some forms of behaviour to be beyond the pale, but it can help shape the choices that people make.

The second response to the dilemma about the morality of displacement is that displacement is actually a sign of success.

It may well be true that CCTV cameras in a city centre tend to push muggers into the surrounding areas without reducing the total amount of crime committed. The flipside of this complaint is that, if CCTV cameras didn't work, there'd be no reason for muggers to move. Instead of seeing displacement as evidence of weakness, then, one might see it as further evidence that crime-fighting is a never-ending game of cat and mouse; that there are no final victories to be achieved here, only temporary advances and retreats.

Whatever the moral dilemmas created, and however reasonable the recognition that some displacement is inevitable, the fact that displacement can and does happen is one of the principal reasons why robbery is among the hardest crimes for a police service to combat. Think about this from an aspirant robber's point of view. He operates in a target-rich environment: there are literally millions of homes and stores and cars and restaurants, to say nothing of ordinary pedestrians, from which he can choose. His *modus operandi* is also disarmingly simple. He takes a gun or knife or heavy object, and threatens harm to the person whose property he wants. Then he makes good his escape. Usually he doesn't have to do more than threaten violence, partly because South Africans know that a significant proportion of criminals really will do the terrible things they say they will.

In circumstances like these, trying to prevent robbery from happening is a mug's game. Security can seldom be improved to the point where no motivated criminal, no matter how audacious or vicious, would ever contemplate committing the crime. Besides, when the security of some targets is raised, others become more attractive. The result is that the prevention of robbery in general is much less feasible than the prevention of any particular robbery: since criminals will tend to look for opportunities that minimise risk and maximise reward, finding ways to increase risk (as tracker devices do) or reduce rewards (as dye-staining technology in cash-in-transit vans' bags does) can reduce the likelihood of a particular crime's being committed. What it may also do, however, is transfer a large proportion of the risk onto others.

*

If a robbery is difficult for the police to prevent, it is usually just as difficult to investigate.

From the point of view of an investigating officer, the essential challenge posed by a robbery is that it is almost always committed by someone who is a stranger to his victim, leaving the detective precious little on which to base the identification of a suspect. In all but a tiny minority of cases, witnesses and victims cannot give an even remotely useful description of the attackers, much less a name, address or license plate number. Usually, all the cops get are broad demographic and physical attributes – age and race, height and weight – and some not very helpful descriptions of the clothes worn, details which, in any event, have to be treated with some scepticism because witnesses are seldom all that reliable. After the restaurant robbery I described in the opening pages of this book, for instance, some of the patrons and staff in the restaurant described Pointy Face as wearing a green hat that shaded his eyes even though I was convinced it was blue skullcap that perched on his head; later, when I met with a police identikit artist, she simply refused to believe that anyone could have as pointy a chin as the one I wanted her to draw.

On the depressingly rare occasions when the police do strike it lucky, fingerprints or DNA are left behind by criminals. But, the CSI television franchise notwithstanding, it is unusual for cops to lift prints that are unambiguously those of the suspect and that are also clear enough to use. This is partly because of poor crime-scene management, which sometimes means cops themselves disturb the evidence, and partly because of the shortage of fingerprint experts. But it is also because a great many robberies happen in public places where the vast majority of fingerprints found have been left innocently by people not connected with the crime. A street mugging, which is by far the most common form of robbery, offers the police almost no prospects for a viable fingerprint. Neither does a hijacking, unless the car is recovered quickly. Matters are a little different with home robberies, which is why this is often the crime of the desperate amateur.

Even when prints belonging to perpetrators are found, they are only really helpful if existing records include the name of their owner and, even better, a reasonably current physical address. Without these, all a lifted print offers is the prospect that, if the perpetrator is arrested for another crime at some future stage, the record of his prints will link him to crimes committed at other times and in other places. The process of linking prints to people was far harder five years ago when the police still used a manual system for identifying fingerprints, and the automation of this process through a digital fingerprint identification system has dramatically improved matters. But fingerprints are only very seldom the sole basis on which people are arrested and charged with robbery. In fact, despite the forensic and investigative technology available, most robbers who are prosecuted have been caught red-handed in the course of their crime or shortly thereafter. Whatever physical and eyewitness evidence is used to prosecute them, it is seldom the basis of the arrest. That, more usually, is made when a police officer, security guard or civilian notices something suspicious and acts on it. Holmes-like sleuthing is not the primary platform on which convictions are based.

The result of all of these difficulties, together with problems in the Detective Service about which I will have more to say later, is that conviction rates for robbery are extremely low. The best study of this was conducted by Ron Pashcke for the South African Law Commission. Looking at three months' worth of crimes, he sought to establish how many had led to successful convictions in the following 18 months. In the case of aggravated robbery, he found that 3% had resulted in conviction and a further 2% were in court at the time. Because of the lack of clues, the vast, vast majority had been closed and were no longer being investigated.

These figures, it must be added immediately, actually overstate police success because of the large number of cases that go unreported or unrecorded. The odds, therefore, on someone being convicted of robbery are substantially less than one in twenty.

Shockingly low as it sounds, a single-digit conviction rate for robbery is hardly unique to South Africa: figures are difficult to compare satisfactorily, but it seems that while a country like the United States maintains a conviction rate for robbery of around 20%, in England and Wales it is well under 10%.

All of which proves a fundamental truth of policing: crimes committed by strangers are hard to solve. If this were not true, it is doubtful that we would have the kind of robbery problem that we do.

*

Robbery, then, is devilishly difficult to police: the number of targets out there and the adaptability of criminals makes the prevention of robbery almost impossible, while the difficulties associated with making cases, means that conviction rates are low. It is not enough, however, to note the reasons why robbery is hard to police and expect that to stand as an explanation for the epidemic of robbery that we've seen over the past decade or so. The difficulties the police face are the same everywhere, after all, but it is not as if they lead everywhere to equally serious crime waves. What, then, distinguishes us from other countries? Why do we have the most serious armed robbery crisis on the planet? The answer, I think, is that robbery is a species of violence and South Africa has a peculiarly – possibly uniquely – violent criminal culture. Our basic problem, in other words, is that there is a terrifying amount of violent energy in our society. It has built up over decades and, like the electricity in a Johannesburg thunderstorm, it is discharged in acts of sudden and sometimes spectacular violence. However hard we work to secure ourselves, the fact is that there are motivated offenders out there looking for opportunities, many of whom are willing to use as much violence as necessary to overcome whatever security systems we have in place or whatever resistance we offer. The problem is not how much security – private and public – we are able to deploy, it is that there are too many people out there willing – even eager – to commit these kinds of crimes. That, in a sentence, is the challenge of bringing down our robbery rates. Stefaans was right: our best bet is to lock the fuckers up afterwards.

Obviously, our pent-up violence is not released only in robberies. Most violent crime is committed by people who know each other. So, before looking at the reasons why there is so much violent energy out there, I want to look at another of its manifestations – our well-known problem of violence committed against women and children.

CHAPTER FIVE

KILROY WAS HERE:
VROUMOER IN SOUTH AFRICA

Read anything about crime in South Africa – from official government policy to the crudest 'commentary' in the tabloid press – and one common theme you'll find will be that of the way South African men treat their children and womenfolk.

There was a time when some people I know would have reacted in horror at the infantilisation of adult women implicit in the assertion that the needs and problems of women and children were somehow the same. A strange coincidence in the thinking of some feminists (who insist that a war is being waged against South Africa's women to keep them in their place) and South Africa's unreconstructed patriarchs (who think that the biological handicaps of women mean they must be treated with greater care by society) has persuaded policymakers and law enforcement officials that women are a bit like children, at least insofar as they are both 'vulnerable groups'. Whatever the differences in the routes by which people with differing attitudes to the empowerment of women have arrived at this conclusion, there is no doubt that the level of crime against women and children in South Africa is a national disgrace. Why this is so is not all that obvious, however.

★

In the most authoritative study of its kind, a team of researchers from the Medical Research Council reviewed nearly 3 300 cases in which women had been murdered during 1999. They found that in cases in which the perpetrator had been identified, fully 50% of all femicides were committed by someone who was a present, former or rejected spouse or lover.

This is a striking and disturbing statistic, suggesting, as it does, that South African women confront very real dangers in the home, and that the men in their lives – people from whom they are entitled to receive far, far better treatment – are responsible for much of the violence committed against them. But, as even the authors of that report note, this is actually not all that unusual. Citing the typically imprecise conclusions of a global study into 'intimate partner femicide', they note that 'the murder of women by an intimate partner accounts for 40–70% of all female homicides.' What is unique to South Africa, then, is not that a large proportion of murdered women were killed by lovers and ex-lovers, but that there were more of these crimes committed per day and per capita than was the case elsewhere. As the study rather sensationally puts it, South Africa had 'the highest [per capita] rate [of intimate femicide] that has ever been reported in research anywhere in the world.'

Before we conclude that these statistics prove there is a war being waged on women in South Africa, there is an important qualification we need to note: we live in a desperately violent country and, if anything, the statistics suggest that when it comes to being murdered, women have it quite easy.

In 2005, the last year for which these figures are available, the national murder rate was nearly 40 per 100 000. Of the 18 500+ dead, however, women and girls, who make up fractionally more than 50% of the population, accounted for about 13% of the dead. The result is that the murder rate for women, at about 10 per 100 000, is less than one seventh the murder rate for men. In fact, if we return to the (admittedly flawed) World Health Organisation study on violence referred to in an earlier chapter, what is striking is that, while a woman in South Africa was about three times more likely to be murdered than the average for women all over the world, South African men were more than six times more likely to be murdered than their brothers elsewhere. Men in this country, it seems, are much more inclined to murder each other than they are to murder women, and they do so phenomenally frequently.

Murder, of course, is only one kind of violence, and women face non-lethal forms of violence that men generally do not. It is wrong to assume that because South Africa's women have been spared the full force of our epidemic of homicide, that all is well on the violence-against-women front. It isn't.

*

There is no way in the world to compare countries' varying levels of domestic violence or to be sure, therefore, that violence in the home is worse here than it is elsewhere. Everything I have read on the subject, however, suggests we do have a particularly severe problem of violence in the home. So much so, that legislation was passed to spur improvements in the police response to the plight of victims of domestic violence. These improvements include exhortations – they fall a long way short of being instructions – that the police adopt a more aggressively pro-arrest orientation when called to the nation's troubled homes. The law also suggests – again, it does not instruct – that cops seek out other ways to help the complainant, such as getting her out of the house or arranging counselling support. The same law creates an innovative legal remedy, the protection order. This is something like a suspended warrant of arrest issued at the request of a victim of domestic violence. It compels police officers to arrest the person named in the order if he violates its terms, even if the underlying act would not ordinarily be regarded as something that should result in an arrest. So wide is the net cast, it covers a great many acts which fall somewhat short of a dictionary meaning of the word 'violence'. These include emotional abuse (like making 'repeated threats to cause emotional pain'), economic abuse ('the unreasonable deprivation of financial resources which the complainant requires'), verbal abuse ('repeated insults and name-calling') and psychological abuse ('obsessive possessiveness'). These are all now deemed acts of domestic 'violence' and could justify the issuing of a protection order and the potential arrest of someone who repeated the act.

To say the least, this definition of domestic violence and the role of the police in managing it extends beyond the boundaries of the typical police officer's conception of his job. It is also largely beyond the skill and resources of the Police Service. Nor is it inconceivable that some would find decidedly odd the idea that law enforcement agencies – by definition, institutions of coercive state power – should play so intrusive a role in relationships shaped by the unfathomable logic of the human heart. Is this, one might ask, really the proper role of government? Of the police? But this objection, which might be made on the basis of a sophisticated, if conservative, liberalism is not the real source of most officers' doubts about the nature of the role set out for them in the Domestic Violence Act. These have their roots in a much less defensible view about the proper place of women in the home and, extending from that, an implicit acceptance of the legitimacy of some male-on-female violence. In this, cops share the patriarchal attitudes that radiate through our national culture, and it is these that explain much about the nature of the violence women face: for all too many men, the women in their lives are to be treated as subjects, in a very feudal sense, rather than as self-directed agents. And, as subjects, they might be targets of legitimate male rage when they are disobedient or disappoint in some other way. Indeed, it wasn't so long ago that South African law recognised the husband as the legal head of the family and authorised the 'reasonable chastisement' of an obstreperous wife.

Domestic violence, in other words, is a manifestation of male attitudes to women in a country in which violence is depressingly common. Like robbery, it is a species of a more general problem of violence, this time coinciding with troubling attitudes to women. Nor is it domestic violence alone that flows from this; the same is true of other sexual crimes.

★

In the past ten years, I have spent quite a lot of time with police officers. In 1998, I followed detectives around for three months, recording their views about the transformation of policing. In 2000, or so, I spent ten days with a detective in the hijacking investigation unit based in Johannesburg. And, in 2003, I spent a year with cops in 12 stations across the country. Each of these experiences, combined with the occasional night out with one or other police unit, has provided ample opportunity for seeing some pretty appalling things. But the most sickening moment I have had in the company of one of our law enforcers didn't involve something I saw. It was something he told me.

I was driving with Superintendent 'Buddy' Badenhorst, the roly-poly commander of the Maluti Police Station deep in the mountainous borderlands between Lesotho and the old Transkei. Buddy was a big man, nearing the end of a long career in the police and, I subsequently learned, he was writing a local version of Harry Potter in isiXhosa. Age and diminishing prospects for promotion hadn't slowed Buddy: he was as committed an officer as I met, a man of passionate enthusiasms. He was taking me on a tour of the district, hauling his ageing bakkie up the mountain passes to the border post and through shaded valleys that crouched in alpine shadows that were a dozen shades of green. As we drove, I asked him about Maluti and the kinds of crimes that dominated his landscape. We'd talked about stock theft and the violence that sometimes comes of it, the occasional *muti* killing, and of the petty squabbles that could erupt into less petty violence. Drug smuggling across the border, a crime he said he knew his officers were involved in, was also a worry. And then he told me that for him, the most difficult cases were the child rapes.

'Were there many?' I asked.

'Not so many. But they stick with you. They make you feel dirty.'

I could well believe this, but I asked him to tell me about the kind of thing he meant. 'A couple of years ago,' he replied, 'we picked up a case of a man who'd raped a little girl. She was three or four. A victim that young doesn't really know what has happened to her. But she was hurt. Bleeding. So we arrested the suspect – someone from the same village – and took him to the station. I take a personal interest in a case like that. I want to interview the suspect myself to make sure the job is done right and that the confession is strong.

'We talked about the crime and I asked him what he did and why. He admitted the sex and when I asked him why he did it, he told me that she wanted it. He said that at first he could hear that she was in pain, but that after a little bit, she started to enjoy herself.'

At the time we spoke, my wife was about two months away from giving birth to a little girl. Whether or not that added to the chill I felt, I cannot say, but I asked the only question I could: 'Did you shoot him?'

'We leave our guns outside when we interrogate,' Buddy replied. 'It was a good thing for him. And for me.'

★

In some ways, the designation of rape and child rape as a sexual crime is controversial. Rape, from one point of view, is not about sex. It is a crime of violence and power. The brute fact that the sexual organs are involved doesn't alter the fact that the primary purpose and effect of the rapist's act is to make his victim suffer. According to this view, the fact that sexual penetration is the method by which the rapist achieves this goal should not be read to mean that the crime is a sexual one: it is a vicious crime of violence and power.

This notion – that rape is not about sex, but about violence and power – is most forcefully conveyed by an expression of Angela Carter's. 'Rape,' she writes, 'is a kind of physical graffiti.' By this, I understand her to mean that the act has less to do with the misguided pursuit of a purely sensual pleasure, than with a more vicious pleasure derived from the damage done to the victim, a pleasure that is directly proportional to the pain that is inflicted. It is as if, by penetrating his victim, the rapist marks out territory. He is asserting something – not ownership, precisely, but at least his ineradicable presence. Rape is not about sex. It is the expression of rage and power, a desire to inflict hurt. The word that insists itself is 'despoilation': Kilroy was here.

While all this is true, it is impossible not to think that rape is also about sex. And it is often about sex between people who have had a relationship with some kind of explicitly or implicitly sexual ingredient. Some of these rapes are committed by men who would never drag a women behind a bush and force themselves on her, but who might believe that the relationship they have with a particular woman should involve (or continue to involve) intercourse. Perhaps this is because they have had sex in the past. Just as likely, it is because he has done what he feels is necessary to have established a legitimate claim on the woman's sexual favours; like a digger on a gold field, he will exercise his 'rights' in any way he must. This doesn't mean that the 'relation-ship' had necessarily lasted for a long period: it may consist of little more than a shared night on the town, a little flirt-ing in the street or just some help with the grocery money. Something as common and ordinary as this might persuade the potential rapist that he is 'owed' sexual services, services he will take whether offered freely or not. 'What does SAB stand for?' a young man on the fringes of criminality asked me once: 'Sex after beer.'

Even in the case of date rape, though, even when the act doesn't involve a gang's dragging a stranger behind a bush, and comes, instead, after a period of flirtation, it is hard not to see it as an expression of an instinct to cause pain, an act motivated by a combination of anger and fantasies of power. Part of the rapist's motivation must be a desire to inflict pain, to punish the victim for withholding what he believes is his due. In his mind he may be teaching her a lesson, even as he is taking what he believes is owed.

This, at any rate, is how I see it. But the motivation for rape may not lend itself to the kind of analysis I am able to offer because it is implicated in so much else in a society – everything from norms of sexuality and courtship, to the structures of our families, and the conflict between a popu-lar culture that stimulates every excitement and an equally pervasive religious morality that denies them. It is far from obvious how one might disentangle everything that is going on here, so explanations for our extraordinary levels of gender-based violence do not come easily to hand. But, if I had to offer an explanation, the starting point would be the way apartheid systematically emasculated and humili-ated the majority of men, some proportion of whom would turn the resulting rage and resentment about their power-lessness into violence against the only people weaker than themselves.

This is, I think, a plausible factor in some of the violence against women and children, but it invites the obvious re-joinder that violence in the home or against women isn't confined to disempowered men from black communities. Something else must, therefore, be going on. That some-thing, I think, is the way in which violence has penetrated our national consciousness, how its sheer ordinariness, its frequency and commonplace-ness means it is all too easy for anger to spill over into violence. That this should hap-pen so often in the home is not surprising since we spend so much time there. Besides, however much we might wish it were otherwise, family life is shot through with stresses and tensions. Nor is it surprising that violent, rage-filled men will pick targets who are weaker than themselves. They may be violent, but they aren't necessarily stupid. Not in that way, at least.

But why is violence so pervasive? Why has it become so much a part of the spirit of our time and place? The time has come to try to answer that question.

CHAPTER SIX

A COUNTRY UNHINGED

What is it that stops one person from robbing or killing another?

This is, admittedly, a cynic's question. But consider it for a moment. What is it that prevents me from killing the guy who takes my parking place at work or looks at my wife funny or just seems fishy? What stops me from putting a knife to someone's belly, demanding his wallet and gutting him if he even looks like refusing?

When it comes right down to it, there are only a couple of respectable answers to this question. One is the fear of hellfire: if our churches are to be believed, doing nasty things to other people will come back to bite you in a big way. Another is conscience, Freud's internal tormentor who punishes our actions so efficiently, we may suffer its punitive sting just imagining ourselves committing a bad deed. A third is fear of earthly punishment: if we rob or kill, we think, we will be caught and punished; we'll spend years in jail, our families will be shamed.

Arguably, these three answers then boil down to one: the fear of consequence.

Whether it is to be visited on us by others or by ourselves, whether the punishment is in this world or the next, one perfectly legitimate reason not to kill is fear. Another answer to this question – perhaps the only other one – is that we don't do these things because we know that people deserve better. Why we think this is uncertain: maybe it's because we have evolved to understand, in unconscious, pre-rational ways, that we do better as a species if we are able to work together; maybe it's because we have an inherent morality of some kind; maybe it's because it's what our parents and our schools and our churches have taught us. However we came by this view, however it was propagated through our culture, is much less important than the fact that we have it.

So we refrain from crime for one or both of two intimately related reasons. The first is that we fear the consequences. The second is that we think that it just isn't a very nice thing to do.

What would happen, though, if a sizable group of people in a society discovered that these reasons are … shall we say, contrived? That, because they are cultural facts, rather than part of nature, they can be defied?

What if they were to discover, in other words, that, when closely examined, there really isn't all that much to back up either the threat of punishment or the necessity to be nice? That the foundations of the taboos against robbing and killing are built in shifting sands? That all that stands between an individual's rage and its violent expression is a set of courtesies and conventions?

These questions are disturbing because they suggest that law-abiding citizens are engaged in an act of collective self-delusion, misrecognising the fact that there may be no real reason to refrain from crime. And yet, a basic, profoundly important criminological fact is that the vast majority of people, including the vast majority of those whose demographic profile makes them most likely to do so, do not commit serious crimes.

Explaining why some people choose criminality is astonishingly hard, more so if the task is to explain why South Africans do this so much more frequently than others. One reason for this, as I tried to explain earlier, is that the patchiness of crime data from the developing world means that we cannot be absolutely certain that our problems are as unique as we sometimes suppose. We simply do not know whether people in Jamaica and Venezuela and Pakistan and Nigeria are much less violent than we are. If they aren't, if South Africa is not all that exceptional, there'd be no need to find causes unique to South Africa to explain our crime levels. This task must remain on the agenda, however, because the fact is that the vast majority of countries, including the poorest ones with the most horrible histories, really do seem to be much less violent than South Africa. But this generates a whole new set of challenges because there are no explanations for the level of violence in South Africa that seem really adequate to the job. Each has much to teach us, but none seems entirely satisfactory.

*

The textbook account of the roots of present-day violence in South Africa goes something like this:

Over the past 350 years or so, state power in this part of the world has been exercised exclusively in pursuit of the interests of a small minority. It has operated with the raw logic of the jungle: the strong dominated and everyone else had to bow down or be destroyed. The roots of this model of state power lie in the 17th century with the arrival of the first Europeans, but the process accelerated in the 19th century when colonists in the Cape extended their presence up the east coast and into the interior. In doing so, they used violence that was at once state-sanctioned and state-building to reshape the social, economic and political realities of the region. If anything, levels of institutionalised violence only worsened during the 20th century as the systems of migrant labour and apartheid were built and then consolidated. In the process, traditional society was ripped apart, turning whole generations of people into disenfranchised units of labour, disembodied hands and arms and backs and legs, with no more rights than a cart horse.

The gist of this account of the roots of crime is that the violence used in the shaping of modern South Africa has not dissipated; it lingers on as a kind of background radiation, deforming and dementing us even as the forms in which it is expressed have mutated. 'The past is never dead,' William Faulkner wrote. 'It isn't even past.'

But it is not just in the grand violence of conquest and submission – something common, surely, to all societies – that the origins of present-day violence are to be found, but in the details of the way that this power was exercised here, and the ways that this differed from other places and other times. In this, as the historian and criminologist Gary Kynoch has observed, what distinguishes apartheid and its predecessors from other colonial experiences was the nature of the institutional architecture on which it was premised: the mining hostels and the prisons. In these spaces, men, torn from the bosoms of their families, lived in a pressure-cooker world where the resort to violence to protect oneself and one's property was common, accepted and necessary. The emergence of gangs was inevitable, as was the legitimisation of violence and the transfer of its skills, processes that have shaped life in South Africa's urban townships ever since. In other colonial settings, by contrast, men worked where they lived, and the emergence of a violence-rich male subculture was much less pronounced.

Apart from the devaluation of human life implicit in the building of apartheid, apart also from the destruction of family and communal life it entailed, apartheid, because it denied the majority their freedom, was a system that could never renounce violence. Whether it was the policeman looking at passes or the urban planner plotting the removal of a 'blackspot', apartheid was premised on the sustained threat of coercive force. This was an essential by-product of the system, a greenhouse gas that was being pumped into the air and was changing the chemical composition of the atmosphere. Violence became part of the ambience of a society in which it was understood by everyone, even by those who denied it, that a small minority lived the good life only because it kept its boots firmly on the necks of everyone else.

Apartheid, then, produced violence in the same way that industrialisation produced and produces global warming – inevitably, insidiously and, now that we know better, cynically, too. It also taught anyone who was paying attention

that one could do anything to secure one's material interests: any oppression could be inflicted if those with the
power felt so inclined. Apartheid, it might be said, was a
kind of raw Darwinism in which the only criterion by
which a policy was to be judged was whether it advanced
the needs of those with the power to institute it; moral rules
were for everyone else.

Needless to say, this is not the kind of lesson law-makers
should teach their subjects unless they are prepared to hold
on to power forever.

If apartheid was premised on pervasive violence, both
implicit and explicit, resistance to apartheid, by taking
millions of children out of school and putting them on
the frontline of the struggle, by legitimating the use of
violence and teaching many its techniques, poisoned the
same well. Noble as the cause might have been, honour-
able as most of its activists undoubtedly were, the violence
of resistance was a crucial element of the country's ambience, its social atmosphere. Nor was it just the technology
and techniques of violence that resistance contributed.
More subtle contributions included the inevitable and
justifiable building up of resentment that was both the
origin of resistance to apartheid and its fuel. But resentment, in the absence of catharsis, is a volatile compound,
one that corrodes everything it touches. It, too, is part of
our heritage.

To the nature of apartheid and the resistance it engen-
dered, accounts of present-day violence often add a third
element: the disappointments of democracy.

Today, millions live on the margins of the formal economy,
their hopes and expectations unmet and arguably unmeetable,

even as the white community continues to dominate the economy along with an 'emerging' middle class. Everyone from the president down warns that those who have been left out will not be patient forever: owing nothing to a society that has given them nothing, some have already lost patience.

There have been other disappointments, too: urbanisation has left our cities struggling to cope with new demands; family structures have buckled and been swept away by a ghastly AIDS epidemic; the housing backlog has left millions of people living in quarters so cramped it is hard to see how they could develop an appreciation of their own rights to the integrity of their bodies, much less the rights of anyone else.

The fruits of liberation have not all been sweet.

These, then, are the basic building blocks of any reasonable account of the causes of crime. At root, the argument is that some a kind of learnt savagery – the product of history and broken homes, sclerotic labour markets and broken souls – has driven a frustrated, angry fraction of South Africans into a life of crime. Indeed, by this reading, levels of violence are almost a metric of the injustices and cruelties of the past, and a gauge of the extent to which the process of social and economic transformation is still unfinished.

There is much truth in this story, and a white writer with no personal experience of the sharp end of apartheid ought to be humble about these matters. Nevertheless, it is hard not to think that, however strong is the case that apartheid preceded and must have caused our violence problem, as it stands, the case isn't strong enough.

★

One reason why the apartheid-did-it explanation doesn't completely satisfy is that South Africans are not unique in the world in having gone through long periods of disenfranchisement, oppression and collective violence. It is hard, in fact, to think of any society on earth that suffered no period of massive trauma of some kind, with most having done so in the comparatively recent past. The Poles and the Chinese, the Koreans and the Rwandans, the French and Vietnamese and Russians and Algerians: pretty much every nation on the planet outside of North America spent some portion of the 20th century on its knees, the victim of catastrophic violence directed either by local tyrants or by foreign overlords.

And yet, only a handful has levels of violence that even approach ours.

Consider Latin America, with its military juntas and its thousands of 'disappeared', its Maoist Shining Paths and its Reaganite Contras. There is much in the history of the countries of that continent that is similar to our own. Indeed, in some cases, their stories – from a quantitative point of view – are far more bloody. Take, for example, tiny El Salvador, where a 12-year civil war through the 1980s saw 75 000 people die out of a population of less than five million. In his book, *The Massacre at El Mozote*, a careful reconstruction of the slaughter of hundreds of people by government forces in December 1981, Mark Danner recounts how the war was marked by the 'mutilated corpses that each morning littered the streets of El Salvador's cities.' Some of the bodies, he writes, 'were headless or faceless, their features having been obliterated with a shotgun blast or an application of battery acid; sometimes their limbs were missing, or hands and feet were chopped off, or eyes gouged out; women's genitals were torn and bloody, bespeaking repeated rape; men's were often found severed and stuffed into their mouths.'

This kind of hyperbolic violence – far greater in absolute, annual and per capita terms than the direct violence of apartheid and resistance in South Africa – has created a society with high levels of violence and a deeply entrenched, peculiarly violent gang culture. Even so, its murder rate, estimated in 2002 at 38 per 100 000, was still at least 10% lower than South Africa's at that time. And, in this, El Salvador is an exception rather than the rule: most Latin American countries have gone through periods of intense repression or outright civil war of the Salvadorian kind, but most have less violence – often far, far less – than South Africa. It may be that this is because the consequences of the centuries of racial humiliation and disenfranchisement in South Africa are different from those left from a brief civil war. But it is not as if the troubles in Latin America were brief spasms of violence disrupting otherwise stable, reasonably just social systems. In El Salvador itself, a civil war in the 1930s had left 12 000 dead. Besides, it seems clear that Latin American societies, like our own, must have had deep, long-term structural features that were painfully oppressive and unjust. How else can one explain the fact that, having revisited the Bible under the banner of Liberation Theology, large swathes of the Catholic priesthood – hardly a body of men traditionally thought of as knee-jerk radicals – felt confident that Jesus himself would have endorsed revolutionary activity? Whether one agrees with their assessment or not, it would not have happened if hacienda capitalism and political autocracy did not make for societies premised on profound injustice.

And this is the problem: if we are to rely on the injustices and oppressions of our history to explain present-day violence in South Africa, we need to show either that all societies with histories of violent oppression and exploitation have similar legacies – something which is patently not the case – or that there was something about apartheid that made it so much more damaging to the moral wellbeing of its subjects. We also need to show why, 13 years after the installation of our democracy, we still suffer its ill-effects. It is far from obvious how this is to be done. Still, only an apologist for apartheid would argue that our past is not a principal reason for the problems of the present. What matters, however, is that it can only ever be a part of the answer. This may actually be a good thing for, as Robert Guest points out in his book on Africa, history is a bit like geography. You can't change it.

*

Apart from our history, attempts to explain violence in South Africa tend to focus heavily on our current socioeconomic indicators, themselves an effect of that history.

We all know that far too many South Africans live lives of misery and desperation. The wretchedness of their conditions, so the argument goes, means that many lives are rich only in humiliation, helplessness and the petty cruelties that keep people awake at night, angry and resentful. The result is a build-up of rage that must sometimes be discharged. For the most part, it is the people nearest to them who suffer; often enough, though, their rage is directed at strangers.

One problem with this became obvious to me in 1999 when I was doing a ride-along with cops who arrested a man for dealing in hijacked vehicles but who also had a full-time job at a sports-marketing company in Rosebank. Another is that Limpopo is our safest province but is also one of the poorest. A third is that there isn't as much support for the proposition that poverty causes crime in the international criminological literature as you might expect. This may be because crime statistics from the developing world are hopeless, but the reality is that, when not suffering a civil war, the majority of countries that are poorer than South Africa are also much less violent. Besides, even if one could show that poorer places tended to have more crime, there would still remain the difficult question of whether poverty caused crime, crime caused poverty (by deterring investment and chasing away those rich enough to move), or if both were caused by something else. This is why academic criminologists cast doubt on any simplistic linkage between poverty and criminality.

By contrast with the lack of consensus about the links between poverty and crime, however, there is a much stronger conviction among academics that inequality causes crime; that the difference between what the rich and poor earn matters more than the depth of poverty. The data used to support this consensus, it must be said, are the same dodgy crime statistics that failed to show a link between poverty and crime, so there may be reasons for doubt here, too. But the intuition is plausible: the fact of inequality could create raw resentments against which experience of the world grates, breeding humiliation and rage. How this could lead to crime and violence needs no sophisticated psychological theories.

For these reasons, inequality is frequently identified as a major cause of crime in South Africa because, as almost everyone knows, our Gini coefficient, the standard measure of inequality, is among the highest in the world. 'Aha!' you can almost hear criminologists exclaim, 'That's why we're so plagued by criminality.' If we are one of the most unequal societies in the world, we should expect to have the highest rates of crime, too.

But there's a problem.

The Gini coefficient is a measure of income inequality: it measures how concentrated income is in the hands of those who earn the most. By this measure, South Africa is one of the most unequal societies in the world. But, by third world standards, South Africa is also a country with a phenomenally well-developed welfare state. In fact, we stand apart from many – possibly most – developing countries in that public expenditure actually ameliorates inequality rather than worsening it. Here, after you factor in the tax that high-income earners pay and the benefits that the poor receive from government, levels of inequality actually fall. This is quite different from many other developing countries where the social contract is that the rich pay no taxes and the poor receive no services.

The inequality-causes-crime argument, therefore, needs some qualification. One way to do this might be to argue that our welfare state is new and so the reduction in inequality has not yet had an effect on crime rates. Another approach might be to focus on asset inequality rather than income inequality. Both of these qualifications may make a more satisfactory case, but somehow they feel like patch-up jobs, the kind of *ad hoc* reasoning that give social scientists a reputation for finding ever more elaborate defences for pet theories that are contradicted by the facts.

There is, in relation to the inequality-causes-crime argument, an even more serious problem. This is that a large body of economic thinking suggests that the widening of inequality is one of the inevitable by-products of rapid economic growth in developing countries. There is no universal consensus on this, but if inequality really does tend to widen as economies expand, then we had better hope that it is not the principal reason we're so violent because it isn't going to get better soon.

*

Apart from poverty and unemployment, there are more prosaic features of the South African landscape that are sometimes invoked by people seeking to explain violence. Two of the more common of these are alcohol and firearms.

There is a great deal of evidence that alcohol is implicated somehow in this country's crime problems. Station Commissioners across the country complain that shebeens generate much of their precincts' crime because whether as victims or perpetrators, drunks make up a substantial portion of the tide of people washing through police stations every weekend. That alcohol should do this is unsurprising since its pharmacological effect is to suppress the neurotransmitters in a drinker's brain that would normally generate the anxiety and fear that inhibit aggression. So, pumped full of Dutch courage, drinkers start more trouble than they should. Drinking patterns in South Africa worsen the effect because we have among the highest rates of alcohol consumption per drinker in the world, as well as a tendency to binge.

Alcohol's use and abuse, then, is a real problem.

But what, we must ask, is an honest policy-maker to do with that knowledge? You can't ban drinking without encouraging the growth of organised crime. Just ask Al Capone. Nor is it obvious that the problem of alcohol can be improved by better regulation: this is an industry in which regulation was abandoned decades ago, an industry in which the ungoverned logic of *laissez faire* has become part of its social DNA. Besides, there are good reasons why temperance advocates should think twice before seeking to deprive people of one of their preferred consolations.

Guns are another matter. This is a technology that allows even the least physically imposing people – individuals like Pointy Face and his young apprentice – to intimidate their victims. For this reason, most people recognise the need for some form of regulation, if only to ensure that criminals have no access to firearms. The trouble is that in a country in which a large proportion of violence occurs between people who know each other, and where conviction rates are too low to be sure that criminal records are an accurate census of who is dangerous and who is not, there can be no bright line separating 'ordinary, law-abiding citizens' from 'criminals'.

107

There is little doubt that too many people with anger-management issues have access to a firearm or that this means that when they do explode, the incident tends to be more lethal than it would otherwise be. And yet, as a society, we remain fascinated by guns, an unhealthy attitude given the rage that poisons so many people.

It may even be that the link between rage and gun ownership is closer than that. Perhaps our rage and our anger-management problems are the source of our fascination with weaponry: a gun, like a lottery ticket, may be a license to dream.

★

It would be no surprise to me if the majority of people who read the preceding section felt that the over-reliance on the guns-and-alcohol effect to explain violence in South Africa is unsatisfactory. Guns are merely instruments, after all. They translate a desire to cause harm into actual bloodshed more efficiently than other tools. What they cannot do is explain the desire itself. Pointing to the abuse of alcohol is a similar form of question-begging. Why, we should ask, do South Africans drink the way we do? And, when we drink, why are our tempers so explosive?

These are the questions to which the standard account of the causes of violence provides some answers: we are a troubled people because our history is one of violence and oppression; people have been pummelled for so long by forces so infinitely more powerful then they are, their souls are raw and sore.

The problem, I have tried to argue, is that this account is

not entirely satisfactory; its reasons don't seem to be reason enough. More than this, the expansion of violence in post-apartheid South Africa makes it hard not to feel cheated by an explanation that relies only on the politics and economics of our history and ignores the here and now. It feels like an abdication of responsibility.

Another kind of answer to these questions, then, focuses on the present. What, it asks, have we done wrong? What are we continuing to get wrong? What have we added to (or taken from) our society that accounts for the eruption of violence, for its becoming an 'everyday abnormality'?

One kind of answer to this question was offered at a public meeting in the posh Johannesburg suburb of Parkview that I attended in the mid-1990s with the then Deputy Minister for Safety and Security, Joe Matthews.

Towards the end of the evening, someone in the audience demanded some commitment that the police would act to stamp out crime in the area. The Deputy Minister, grey and somewhat tortoise-like in aspect, looked at the assembled score-or-so suburbanites and asked what any criminologist knows is a reasonable question: 'Where in the world has a criminal justice system ever stamped out crime?' There was a moment's silence before a voice near the front called out, 'Saudi Arabia.' Within seconds, a chant reverberated through the community hall of this, Johannesburg's twee-est and most liberal suburb: 'Cut their hands off! Cut their hands off! Cut their hands off!'

Stripped of its more objectionable content, the kind of thinking reflected in the chanting of the people shouting at Minister Matthews puts the focus of any discussion about the causes of crime in South Africa on the machinery of law enforcement – the police and courts and intelligence services – whose efforts seem so ineffectual in the face of the onslaught. Where are the bobbies on the beat? people ask. Why do so many get away with murder? The state, so the argument goes, is failing in its primary responsibilities – responsibilities that are implicit in the social contract that forms the basis of a state's legitimacy, and that are its principal purpose.

As with all the other components of this ever-expanding tale, there is something to this, if only because policing and law enforcement do help to shape the world in which we live. At the same time, by some measures South Africa has enough cops. Although it is phenomenally difficult to be sure because there is no universal definition of who counts as a police officer, we think we have about the same number of cops per 100 000 people as the international average. We also spend, by international standards, a large proportion of our national income on criminal justice.

Where our policing strategies have gone wrong is a subject for a later chapter, but, for the moment, it is necessary to register that the ability of our police service – of *any* police service! – to have prevented a crime wave like ours was always going to be more limited than most people believe. This is because imposing order in disordered places is exceptionally difficult. For proof of this, consider America's experience in Iraq, where it has something like 160 000 of its own soldiers working with nearly 100 000 troops from its coalition partners and mercenaries attached to security companies. Given that the Iraqi population is about half that of South Africa's, there are something like two or three times as many security personnel per person in Iraq as there

110

are in South Africa. Add the Iraqi army and police, and the ratio balloons to something approaching six times the South African figure.

To say the least, despite their numbers, these troops have not found imposing order, much less the rule of law, to be especially easy.

South Africa is not Iraq, of course, whatever the BBC might think. For one thing, an insurgency driven by suicide bombers and recently deposed, deeply disaffected national minorities, is not the same thing as a crime wave: when you kill an insurgent, it may very well be that the principal effect is to encourage his brother to take up arms. Besides, the active and partisan involvement of local security forces complicates enormously the law-and-order challenge in Iraq. Neither of these factors, one hopes, is true of our criminal justice system.

These comparisons make our problems seem manageable, but there are other differences between our situation and Iraq's which admit of more disquieting interpretations. One of these is that the rules of engagement of US forces in Iraq are somewhat more robust than those allowed a police service in a democracy: where American soldiers kill suspected insurgents (and anyone they choose to call an insurgent) pretty much at will, cops in South Africa must make arrests and investigate cases in the hope that a small percentage of the suspects they know of will go to jail. As a consequence, South Africa's security services are able to generate much less deterrence than the Americans in Iraq.

Another difference is that an insurgency, however broad-based and however fragmented its leadership, must be more centrally directed than is a crime wave composed of swarms of unconnected criminals. Focused bombing and artillery and snipers could conceivably decapitate an insurgency. They cannot do so here because, despite the *spookstories* to the contrary, the vast bulk of South African crime is not that organised. In the absence of a head, it is hard to see how decapitation (or even a negotiated truce) would be possible.

The lesson of Iraq, then, is that masses of troops and ultra-permissive rules of engagement cannot be made to work even when disorder is relatively organised; that wilfully, obdurately disorderly places are not easily subjected to the rule of law.

The bottom line is that anyone who thinks that the difference between South Africa's crime rate and that of a country like the United Kingdom is just a matter of the numbers, competence or commitment of England's bobbies, is fooling themselves.

There is much we need to do to build our criminal justice system, but there is much else to do, besides. We are not Iraq: our problems and prospects are infinitely better. But, like that benighted country, ours is a half-made land. This is not just because we are scarred by a history of discrimination and racial humiliation, an unequal distribution of wealth and desperate poverty. It is because the rule of law remains at least as much an aspiration as a reality; because we have yet to learn the conventions and civilities, the social graces and the urbane niceties that are assumed in our Constitution; because, though we have slipped off the shackles of oppression, we have not yet built a society that is whole and stable and which knows itself.

★

In a previous chapter I described how context shapes people's choices. Using my experience of sitting in a traffic jam and debating the morality of using the emergency lane, I tried to argue that an individual's decisions are shaped not by his or her values alone, but by the behaviour of other people around them and the context that this creates. The gist was that, as more people break a social norm, others are drawn into doing the same. This is not because social conditions or individual values have changed, but because the norms that we apply when making decisions are conditional, with one of the conditions being what everyone else is doing. If this is so, then, as norm-breaking becomes more common, the changing context draws even people with relatively high levels of resilience into doing what they know is wrong.

Another example of how context shapes decision-making is what happens on the dance floor at a party. Some people who go to parties will dance when no-one else will. Others need someone else to break the ice, but will join in pretty quickly. People like me, on the other hand, will dance only when there are plenty of people already making fools of themselves so that my flailing legs will go unnoticed. The point is that, except for the small minority of extroverts who dance because there's music, as the dance floor fills, one's endowment of inhibition or rhythm may become less and less decisive in determining whether one chooses to dance. There is, in other words, a kind of dance-party chain reaction, so that once it gets going, it sustains itself.

On the opposite side of the moral spectrum from dancing parties, it might be that this kind of runaway reaction –

when people do something because lots of people are already doing so — is the motor that drives mass horrors such as the Rwandan genocide.

If how one behaves is really determined in part by what everyone else is doing, then one of the key factors driving our crime wave may be nothing more than the fact that violence has become so pervasive. One reason for this is that, for all the reasons I've described in this chapter, our history and the nature of our society mean that too many South Africans start off with low thresholds to joining in: many are all too willing to commit violent crimes. Another reason, though, is that the pervasiveness and persistence of this kind of behaviour has dragged others with higher resilience against the temptations of criminality into crime. This it has done by making it easier to rationalise the act ('*everyone* is doing it!') and by conferring on newcomers a kind of herd-immunity ('With so many people doing it, what are the chances that *I'll* get caught?').

A key reason for our level of violence, then, is the effect that existing patterns of crime have had in shaping the choices each of us makes. This might explain why we have extraordinarily high levels violence even though neither our history nor our socio-economic profile is so exceptionally awful as to explain it. Of course it is true that we have inherited a society with a very high potential for crime, one with all the necessary preconditions. But, the meltdown, having started, may now be feeding off its own energy: a fire, as an old expression has it, creates its own wind. Or, to switch metaphors, one might say that the growth and persistence of violent crime has all the cause-and-effect logic of a dance craze.

The great thing about the dance-floor analogy is that it works even if social values do not change. It may be that a good many South Africans were more prone to violence than people in other countries because of our history, but the crime wave can be explained without assuming this. This is because its motive force, which is the crime itself, changes the context within which people make their choices so that, after a tipping point was reached, the crime wave could feed off itself. This may very well have happened decades ago, with only the spilling over of crime into the suburbs being of comparatively recent vintage. It may not be necessary, therefore, to argue that socio-economic factors worsened in the recent past to explain the surge in crime. Nor, strictly speaking, is it necessary to show that values have deteriorated in recent years. All that needs to have happened is that a vicious cycle has developed in which high levels of crime now create the context for further criminality.

I believe that something like this has been a big factor in South Africa. But, it is not as if this excludes the possibility that values did change in ways that were more criminogenic. This, too, may have happened: the values of South Africans may well have become more conducive to criminality than they once were. The argument I want to make about the deterioration of South African values, however, is not the usual one about the conspicuous consumption of the elite, and the way this might have promoted the resentments and jealousies of people without the means. This is an argument that someone from a 'previously advantaged' community should be excluded from making unless and until his community recognises that large portions of its wealth are a consequence of its former privileges, and shows a greater willingness to give it up. Until that happens, decrying the materialism of others seems a little hypocritical. The evils of conspicuous consumption are not, in any case, the source of our change in values. This, I think, is rooted in demographics.

Demographic factors, especially the age structure of the population, have long been recognised as one key to understanding crime rates. The insight that underpins this is that crime, especially violent crime, is committed almost exclusively by young men. As a consequence, societies with relatively large numbers of young people tend to be more violent than others, and societies become more violent as any population bubble passes through the dangerous years between its late teens and late twenties. This is partly a simple fact of demographics – more young men equals more violent crime – but changes in population structure are not just demographic facts. They are cultural ones, too.

*

The difference between a society and an unshaped mass of individuals is that the former exists only when a web of social institutions – from families and government agencies, to schools and churches – knit them together. This is partly a mechanical process of bringing people together to achieve certain practical, productive ends. But it is also a symbolic one in which shared ideas and values are transmitted. Inevitably, the transmission of values happens largely from one generation to the next and it is the mechanics of how this happens that are disrupted as a society's age structure changes

116

and the ratio of older people to younger ones falls. As the cohort of young people grows, relative to the rest of the society, and as the population bubble passes through the dangerous years, it becomes harder and harder for older generations to transmit established values and morality to younger ones using the machinery of a society's existing institutions. The changing ratio of old people to young means that there are fewer parents, teachers, police officers and the like for every child. The effects of this can be enormously disruptive, and this argument has been used persuasively to explain why crime exploded in America in the mid-1960s, at precisely the moment when the first baby-boomers born after the Second World War entered their late teens and early twenties.

Applied to South Africa, this argument offers some important insights about the crime wave we have gone through. Like the United States in the 1960s, ours is a country that has become steadily younger. In addition, exaggerating the effect, the present generation of young men are the children of the 'lost generation', the youngsters who rejected, rebelled against, and ripped apart the hated institutions of apartheid. Having grown up in the ruins of these institutions, it would not be surprising if they have not been especially good at transmitting the kinds of values that a stable society needs.

But demographic change is only one factor affecting the transmission of values. Another is that the death of apartheid meant that much more social and cultural space within which young people could find and assert their selfhood suddenly came into existence. This space was ungoverned by existing norms, largely because existing social institutions

117

had developed before it did. None of them – families, schools, police – was equipped to reproduce community values and to set limits on the potentially dangerous business of young people's quest for selfhood. The result was the troubling spectacle of too many young men, cut adrift from many of the moral bearings that stable institutions provide, having to figure out for themselves what limits to fix on their own behaviour. Needless to say, some didn't set very tight restrictions on what was permissible and, in so doing, weakened the inhibitions on criminality.

Much, I suspect, would have been different if the death of apartheid had been accompanied by an economic boom, if hundreds of thousands of young men had found themselves in gainful employment instead of wasting away the primes of their lives bored and angry. Not only would they have had incomes, but they would have learnt the discipline and self-respect that comes from work. In the event, as a vehicle for positive socialisation, the labour market worked no better than our schools and police service. Instead of finding jobs and a workplace, young men in post-apartheid South Africa entered adulthood in a world that lacked the structures and institutions needed to transmit the kinds of values that help inhibit criminality. Theirs was a half-made world. The law, with its clear distinctions between right and wrong, existed, but, value-wise, there was little to impede the chain reaction of criminality. Worse still, once it commenced, the explosion in crime made the building of new institutions even harder because one of the effects of crime is to tear apart the social fabric even further.

These are, for want of a better word, 'cultural' facts and they are among the most important reasons why crime is so

pervasive and why it is so hard to control: the social infra-
structure we need to defeat criminality has been weakened
by that criminality. The result is that what has driven up
crime and violence is something subtler than our history
and our socio-economic conditions, something less ame-
nable to change than the structure of our society (hard as
that may be). Violence has become a cultural phenomenon.
It is a form of behaviour driven by its own logic and attractive in its own right, one that is, for a significant minority,
an expression of their selfhood, something towards which
young men are drawn by the 'enticement, or incitement, of
peer-group prestige'.

★

Suggesting that violence in South Africa is a cultural phenomenon, like any culture-based argument, is controversial,
even provocative. And yet it seems a much more fruitful
explanation than some of the 'root cause' thinking we've
been offered. It implies, however, that simply implementing
existing policies is unlikely to work by itself. Raising
people out of poverty is a good and noble thing, and it
needs to make no impact on crime to be justified. But the
impact of this on crime will be less an effect of reducing
material need than of the manner in which increased incomes changes the self-concepts of the people whose lives
improve. Economic reality must be remade, but so too must
be the climate in which social conditions are translated by
people into forms of human behaviour.

All this might seem depressing, but, surprisingly perhaps,
an analysis that says that there is no ultimate root cause of

our peculiar crime problems, and that violence has grown through its fashionableness, may be a cause for some hope because, as any marketer knows, fashions change. Social dynamics can be unwound. Think, for instance, of what might happen to a party if all the most extroverted guests were kidnapped: with no-one to get the dancing going and pull others in, everyone could wind up standing against the walls. Perhaps the same is true of crime; perhaps if we can get enough criminals off the streets, other people involved would make different decisions.

I will suggest in a later chapter that this is something we might be able to do if we set up our criminal justice system to come down like a ton of bricks on violent criminals. Before I make that case, though, I need to deal with a potential objection that some readers might raise. Crime, they may argue, is not driven by cultural factors, but by immigrants and organised syndicates. Deal with these, and we will have no crime problem.

CHAPTER SEVEN

A SUNNY SPOT FOR SHADY CHARACTERS OR THE FOREIGN ELEMENT IN OUR CRIME

Late in 2006, I had a conversation with a senior detective at police headquarters in Pretoria. Our meeting was not about organised crime, but he was particularly excited by the success he and his officers had had in rolling up a gang whose modus operandi was to rob supermarkets. Armed with AK47s and a variety of smaller weapons, groups numbering up to twenty would enter a store, tell everyone to get down, and steal all the cash in the registers and safes. In most incidents of this type, no-one was shot, but after one notorious incident in June, four cops, acting on a tip-off, had gone to a house near Johannesburg's CBD to look for people involved in one of these crimes earlier in the day. Unaware that the gang was waiting for them, they entered the house. In the ensuing firestorm, all four were killed along with eight suspects.

'You know what the police are like,' the officer said. 'Unless it involves perlemoen or drugs, no-one thinks that something is organised crime. So what happens? Every time there's a chain-store robbery, the detectives in that area investigate it by themselves. No-one brings all those investigators and their dockets together to make the links. I said that that was rubbish, so we drew 20 dockets from across

Johannesburg and we brought all those investigating officers here for a workshop. The first thing we did was say, "OK, let's see the CCTV pictures from these crimes." And so all the pictures of all the suspects were put on the table. And surprise, surprise, there were a lot of common faces.'

At that point, he hauled out a poster-sized sheet of cardboard. On it was a large matrix, with each column headed by the case number of one of the 20 crimes he'd spoken of. Below these were printed all the usable pictures taken of the men involved. Not only were there common faces that were readily identifiable, but some of the suspects had been considerate enough to wear the same shirts to more than one crime; linking the men to each other and to the various crimes proved quite easy. Then, after a few of the men were captured, it was a matter of persuading them that it was in their own best interests to cooperate. 'Eventually, we arrested nearly fifty people. Since then, there's been almost no incidents.'

*

There is much that is interesting about this story, but for the moment, it is worth dwelling on just one aspect. The officer had introduced his story by saying, 'You know what the police are like. Unless it involves perlemoen or drugs, no-one thinks that something is organised crime.' By this he implied that these robberies were also a form of organised criminality, and had to be dealt with as such. It was a view that corresponded with another I'd heard a few weeks previously, this time articulated by a senior police spokesperson who was being interviewed on the radio following a deadly cash-in-transit heist in Johannesburg. One of the more banal questions put to her was whether the police believed that those involved in the outrage were members of an organised syndicate. 'Yes,' she replied, before going on to explain that the gang had been heavily armed and had had access to a getaway vehicle. 'That kind of sophistication is typical of organised crime.'

I remember thinking when I heard this that this was a definition of organised crime that was so broad as to be empty: a group that has access to high-calibre weapons and possesses the foresight to arrange a getaway car hardly sounds like the kind of sophisticated law enforcement challenge of the kind made famous by Tony Soprano. It suggested that the word 'organised' in the phrase 'organised crime' was being used as an intensifier, a synonym for 'very, very bad'.

Whatever I felt about this issue, though, international treaties on organised crime support the spokesperson's view. The United Nations convention on the subject, signed with some irony in the Sicilian city of Palermo, defines an organised criminal group as one made up of three or more persons who work together for a period of time to commit one or more serious crimes. For the purposes of the convention, a serious crime includes all offences that might result in a jail term of four or more years. The effect is that almost any robbery – from a raid on a chain store to a mugging on the street – could, legalistically speaking, be treated as an act of organised criminality if it involved at least three offenders.

Using a definition that broad, South African crime is very, very organised. But, when most people talk about organised crime, they generally would not have so inclusive a definition in mind. What they would be thinking about – what they have been encouraged to think about – is the nefarious role played by foreign criminal masterminds in South Africa's crime wave.

★

To hear some people tell the tale, South Africa's emergence into the global economy after 1994 was just the opportunity that international criminal groups, desperate for new markets and new trade routes, had been waiting for. Theirs is a tale that generally begins by noting, often with some self-righteousness, that apartheid South Africa lacked the systems and structures needed to combat organised crime. This was a state isolated from the rest of the globe, one that had committed all its resources and energies to defeating a struggle for democracy. Given the existential threat it believed it faced, it was blithely unconcerned about organised crime. Worse, pursuing policies such as sanctions-busting and community destabilisation through support of vigilante groups, it may have actually helped to foster organised crime. This lack of diligence on the part of the police and intelligence agencies in the 1980s meant that the country failed to develop the legal tools and technical skills needed to protect itself from the kinds of threats that emerged after 1994. This was a tragedy, doubly so because the SAS *South Africa* was about to be launched onto the high sees of globalisation, a process that would see the efflorescence of the kind of dense commercial links with other countries that organised crime needs if it is to tranship its contraband or launder its ill-gotten wealth.

The transition to democracy also facilitated the penetration of organised crime into our social formation in other ways. It weakened the state's law enforcement machinery, which was, in any event, exhausted from its long struggles. It was now losing staff and status, and had become distracted by the prickly business of defending itself and its members at the Truth Commission. In addition, the opening of the country's borders created the channels criminal groups needed if they were to insert their members into the country. Finally, South Africa's demobilising militaries – statutory and non-statutory – as well as its established gangs and vast networks of former jailbirds, meant there was talent aplenty from which organised criminal groups could happily recruit.

There may be something to this story, even if it does sound ominously like the opening pages of HG Wells's science-fiction novel, *War of the Worlds*, which describe humanity's complacency before a Martian invasion of late 20th-century earth. No-one, Wells writes, imagined that 'across the gulf of space ... intellects vast and cool and unsympathetic regarded this earth with envious eyes, and slowly and surely, drew their plans against us.'

Attractive as South Africa may have looked to international groups of organised criminals, however, it is hard to believe that these intellects, no matter how vast or cool or unsympathetic, explain more than a small portion of the problem of violence in South Africa. Yes, South Africa would have looked good to groups looking for new smuggling routes for narcotics originating in Latin America or

East Asia, and destined for Europe and America. To senior figures in the world's organised crime groups, the high quality of our amenities combined with the glacial speed of our extradition procedures, might have suggested South Africa would be a happy base from which one might work or to which one might retire. For people like these, this is the best of all possible worlds: apart from the sun, we have a constitution which means that cops won't break down their doors and shoot them (as might happen in other lands), but, at the same time, our justice system is so slow that the process, even when uncorrupted, takes forever. That it is corruptible only makes South Africa more attractive.

Unsurprisingly, senior and not-so-senior crime figures from Italy and Germany and Equatorial Guinea have been drawn to the country. But to think that this kind of migrant is implicated in more than a tiny fraction of the run-of-the-mill crimes which fill our newspapers – the murders and rapes and robberies that cause most public anxiety – is quite far-fetched. Most of them are much happier keeping above the fray, briefing their lawyers over cappuccinos and cake, and getting their fingers into the real money that comes of more-or-less legitimate business activity – smuggling, protection rackets and contract enforcement in the criminal underworld.

Still, if transnational organised crime of this type is not the source of this country's crime problems, it does not follow that foreigners play no role.

★

At the start of this chapter, I described a conversation with a senior detective who told me about the successful rolling up of 50-odd members of a gang that had been terrorising shoppers and shopkeepers in Johannesburg. At the time, I neglected to tell the story's punch-line: 'Every one of the people we arrested,' the officer said, 'was Zimbabwean.'

There is no doubt that foreigners commit crimes – some of them spectacular and vicious – in South Africa. Nigerians, for instance, dominate some of the key niches in the criminal economy, especially the importing of cocaine and heroin, and the street trade in hard drugs in our inner cities. This has led to their involvement in other forms of crime because their clients seldom command stable incomes and many finance their habits through theft and robbery, creating a market opportunity for dealers. Foreigners – especially Zimbabweans and Mozambicans – are also involved in some of the high-profile robberies like cash-in-transit heists and chain-store robberies, and there is more than enough anecdotal evidence to conclude that they also break into houses and steal cars.

The most serious issues arise with those crimes that demand some foreign involvement and which might happen less often but for the presence in South Africa of what the United Nations call 'transnational organised crime'. This is particularly true of the drug trade where the comparative advantages of exotic minorities include language and cultural ties that make it very difficult for law enforcement agencies to penetrate their networks, as well as well-established links with traders in other parts of the world. These advantages mean that they are the industry's natural market-makers. This, one is tempted to say, is as it should be. Certainly, it is like this everywhere from London (where Jamaicans and Nigerians dominate the crack trade) to New York (where Russians and other Eastern Europeans run the protection industry).

Another advantage that foreigners may have is their access to criminal networks (and law enforcement agencies!) in countries like Mozambique and Zambia and Zimbabwe, access that means they are best placed to organise cross-border transactions for cars and drugs and guns. It is true also that the meltdown in Zimbabwe has fuelled crime in South Africa by exporting desperately poor people with few prospects in our economy, but who still have responsibilities for people back home. Nor would it be a surprise to learn that Zimbabwean soldiers, their incomes eroded by hyper-inflation and fearful that a future government might not allow them as close to the trough as they have come, might be supplementing their incomes by the odd foray into a South African bank.

The important point, though, is that these are not the typical migrant to South Africa, and it would be grossly unfair to tar all with the same brush. Still, since most migrants are poor and young and male, many will get involved in crime here. This is not, I suspect, because they come here planning to make a living on the wrong side of the law. Instead, having come here in the (unrealised) hope of a better life, and having experienced the wild and crazy streets of our cities, they may follow the example of those around them, and turn to crime.

Whether they come to the country in order to commit crime or find themselves committing crime despite having come with the intention of finding work, foreigners commit crime in South Africa for the same reasons that South

Africans do, reasons that have to do with social conditions, the quality of law enforcement and the general ambience. It is not as if we would attract a better class of migrant if we got our act together, but we might transform fewer of the potentially decent new arrivals to South Africa into criminals. It is, after all, a long way to come to steal a TV set.

CHAPTER EIGHT

FROM 'FIGHTING CRIME' TO 'FIGHTING CRIMINALS'

The essence of the argument I have been making is that socio-economic conditions in South Africa, though always likely to produce crime, cannot tell us why South African crime is as pervasive and violent as it is. This, I have suggested, is the result of a chain reaction that has seen high levels of criminality lead ever more people copycatting others into crime. This has turned what would have been a serious crime problem into one that has turned violence into something approaching epidemic proportions, a problem far bigger than can be explained solely by the factors – whether historical, social or economic – that are usually deemed to be the 'root causes'.

There is a great deal that needs to be done to turn crime levels around, much of it outside of the realm of criminal justice. But, the criminal justice system is a crucial component of a government's response to high levels of crime and, if we are to bring down crime levels, the police, courts and prisons will have to shoulder much of the responsibility. The question we have to ask is whether present strategies allow them to achieve this. The short answer, I think, is that they do not, largely because the model of policing we have developed is unsuited to our problems.

★

Since 1994, policing in South Africa has been in the thrall of a vision of itself that emphasises the role of the police in preventing crime. 'We are the thin blue line,' every police officer from the topmost managers to the greenest constables says of his job description. 'It is up to us to ensure that crime comes down.'

This idea – that the primary aim and object of policing is the prevention of crime – is part of the constitutional mandate of the SAPS. It is also the driving theme of the White and Green Papers on policing, as well as the National Crime Prevention Strategy. To this list of policy documents emphasising the crime prevention role of the police, we can add the Service's recent operational strategies, as well as the National Commissioner's target for the Service of a 7-10% annual reduction of 'contact crime' (murder, attempted murder, sexual crimes, assault and robbery). In addition, virtually the only number the management of the Police Service seems to care about is the amount of crime recorded at its police stations. This attitude is also reflected in the immodest, pessimistic and nearly fact-free assertion in a recent SAPS annual report that 'the decrease in contact crime achieved in 2005/06 is quite remarkable, given the fact that the generators of and conditions conducive to crime (such as urbanisation, unemployment and poverty, growing material needs and the abuse of alcohol and drugs) probably increased during the period under review'.

Policing, we are told continuously, is not only focused on preventing violent crime, but has been successful even when social and economic variables have moved against it.

There is much to commend in the focus on preventing crime, and a police service that didn't want to engineer a reduction in crime would be a pretty miserable thing. Crime prevention is also an astute choice of focus because it plays well in budget negotiations with the Treasury and Cabinet. The most important reason for the place crime prevention occupies in the Police Service's conception of itself, though, is that cops believe sincerely, almost religiously, that they are society's last, best and only hope. It is how they see themselves and how they understand their work. Nor are they alone in this: it is true also of politicians (in government and in opposition), of every pundit and editorialist, of activists and researchers in the key NGOs, of academics in the most fashionable criminology journals, and of diners in Johannesburg's restaurants. There may be much that divides South Africans, but when it comes to policing, everyone seems to be of one mind: the police need to focus on preventing crime.

But what if everyone is wrong?

*

There are few universally agreed conclusions that emerge from the oceans of paper produced by international studies on the impact of one or other police strategy on the level of crime. Strategies that work in one place or at one time fail in other places or at other times. Something that works to reduce car theft might raise, lower or leave undisturbed the number of burglaries committed. Interventions that reduce bank robberies may leave unaffected muggings that take place on the pavements outside those same banks. And, as described earlier, even when something does work, it often generates displacement: criminals move to other areas or change their *modi operandi* or simply move on to other targets. Add to this the confusion generated by different analysts routinely coming to opposing conclusions using the same data, and it is just about impossible to assert anything about when and how policing might prevent crime. The result, one renowned American student of policing concluded, was that policing's claim to being a profession was radically undermined by the complete absence of a body of established techniques whose impact had been rigorously tested and scientifically established. The usually unacknowledged truth is that the best policing is not like the best medicine or engineering: no-one knows what works, what doesn't, and what the side effects are.

Despite these doubts about what we know, the one thing that appears to be true is that, at its very best, policing can, indeed, prevent crime. But there is a crucial qualification that must be added. Policing can do this only if the scope of the crime problem is narrow, if the challenge isn't to reduce all forms of actual and conceivable crime. The narrowness of focus may be a function of the particular problem's being confined to a small area (a few city blocks, say), or because it consists of crimes committed by a relatively small and readily definable group of offenders (drug dealers and users, for instance), or because the criminals who are being targeted are interested only in a relatively limited, well-defined set of targets. In carefully defined cases like these, policing can make a big difference.

If the problem, then, is mugging in a CBD, closed-circuit cameras or a 'cops on the dots' technique can work. If car theft and hijacking are the priority, then tracking devices and market disruption strategies will make a difference. If there are open-air drug markets, police harassment and clever urban design can drive the problem away.

Though policing can be made to work against specific problems, the flipside is that it is much less effective against generalised crime threats such as ours. Our crime problem is not spatially confined to small areas. Our crimes are not committed by a small, readily identifiable group of offenders. Most importantly, our criminals have unpredictable and eclectic tastes in target, and a demonstrated ability to shift from one target to another in response to changing patterns of reward and security. These factors make our crime problem unsusceptible to most of the tools in policing's toolbox.

All this is proved, rather than refuted, by New York's experience with zero-tolerance policing, a policing philosophy that contends that a police force can reduce serious crime by focusing law enforcement attention on every crime equally, whether it is the most petty (such as graffiti on the subways) or the most serious. This approach, so the argument goes, helps cops net serious criminals as they commit less serious crimes and, more importantly, changes the climate within which would-be criminals decide whether or not to break the law: because jay-walking laws are aggressively policed, convenience-store robbers stay home and watch baseball on TV.

The reality, however, is that New York's crime problems in the early 1990s – especially its murders and robberies – were so heavily concentrated around its open-air drug markets, that dealing with crack and crack dealers had the effect of bringing down city-wide murder and robbery rates by more than half. Zero tolerance, though the official policy of the NYPD, was much less important than the strategy of aggressively policing drug markets, a strategy which coincided happily with the maturation and stabilisation of those markets. In South Africa, where there is no single feature of our crime landscape that drives crime rates in a manner comparable to the effect of crack markets in New York, it simply isn't possible for policing to focus as effectively. There is no single priority, certainly, on which cops could concentrate their efforts that would have the effect of bringing down murder or robbery by half.

Apart from this, visible policing of the sort we usually imagine, is something that only ever works in cities that have much higher population densities than is usual in South Africa. It is futile, for instance, to say that the difference between New York and Johannesburg is that one sees police officers on every corner in the former but never in the latter. New York – especially Manhattan – is a pedestrian city, and a police officer stationed on a city corner will be seen by thousands of people every hour. In South Africa, where our cities sprawl obscenely, the only places where this would be true are our inner cities, our transport hubs and our shopping malls. Everywhere else, a police officer standing on a street corner sees, and is seen by, too few people to make the effort worthwhile. This is especially true of our suburbs, where winding roads and forests of trees reduce visibility dramatically, but even our low-rise and almost treeless urban townships generally have density levels that are too low for efficient visible policing.

If the urban form is the main reason visible policing based on foot patrol and point-duty doesn't work, it also undermines vehicle patrols because cops in cars have too large an area to cover. The result is that the odds of a police vehicle's driving past a burglary while it is in progress, much less actually noticing that a crime is being committed at all, are vanishingly small. The same is true of efforts to catch people on the scene, especially since calls to the police inevitably come too late to prevent the suspect from slipping off. That's why, in a year spent with cops on the beat, I saw only one burglar arrested at the scene of his crime. And the only reason he couldn't escape was that he'd torn his hand so badly while breaking a window, he couldn't climb over the garden wall. His able-bodied partner, on the other hand, was long gone.

These constraints on traditional patrol work have meant that visible policing in South Africa has tended to adopt the much more disruptive methods of roadblocks and cordon-and-search operations. These look good and do have real crime-fighting potential, but unless they are sustained over long periods, something which requires resources that police stations don't have, their impact decays quickly. Nevertheless, it is precisely these tactics that the Police Service has put at the centre of its operational strategies since 1994, and it is these that have attracted the lion's share of resources since the police budget started to grow quickly after the turn of the century.

It is time, I believe, for a strategic rethink.

*

The domination of the idea that policing in South Africa needs to be focused on preventing crime has its roots in the transitional period of the mid-1990s which brought together at the helm of the Police Service a group of people – politicians, their civilian advisors and cops – who shared a vision of policing that set itself in opposition to another that was then, and is now, a plausible alternative: the development of the capacity of the state to find, prosecute and incarcerate criminals.

The interest shown by politicians and their advisors in crime prevention is easy to understand. Among us were people who had been harassed and tortured by cops and who had developed a deep suspicion of policing. We knew also that the approach to policing that had gone before was unsustainable, grossly illegitimate and had to change. Just as importantly, we believed fundamentally that state power ought to be used to do good, and that if people could be prevented from committing crimes, there would be less need to use the state's more coercive powers. Besides, across government, officials understood crime to be a symptom of historical injustices and felt instinctively that a focus purely on punishing criminals would be to add carceral insult to socio-economic injury. Better and more noble, then, to bend all the police's efforts to the prevention of crime rather than the punishment of offenders.

Apart from these instinctive responses, the interest in policing-for-crime-prevention was supported by cutting-edge criminological work then dominating the leading academic and policy journals. This held that policing was everywhere in crisis because of its inability to meet community demands for a reduction in crime, and that it had to change if it were to do so. These were American and British journals, on the whole, and the eighties and early nineties had seen dramatic increases in violent crime in much of the first world, a trend that had cast doubt over traditional police strategies. The result was a broad split in criminologists' thinking about policing. On the one hand, right-wing thinkers were punting 'broken windows' or 'zero-tolerance' policing. On the other, left-of-centre pundits and policy-makers advocated the ill-defined philosophy of 'community policing'. The former envisaged cops' enforcing the law against every offender, however petty the crime; the latter hoped to see police services working closely with others to address the causes of crime through problem-solving exercises involving anyone from drug counsellors to urban planners, from community activists to school' principals.

In practice, advocates both of community policing and of zero-tolerance policing wanted to see the police becoming more proactive, with stepped-up patrol work at the centre of both visions. There were important differences, though, between zero tolerance, which imagined steely-faced law enforcers engaging criminals aggressively, and advocates of community policing, who hoped to develop a model of street policing that might have been termed 'armed social work'. Nevertheless, both approaches were founded on getting uniformed, visible policing to work more effectively, and either might have become a model for police-led crime prevention in South Africa. Given the instinctive distaste for a policing strategy premised on strict law enforcement, however, it was to the advocates of community policing that those of us who'd come into government in 1994 turned.

Whatever the views of civilian policy-makers, though, it was police leadership itself that was decisive in taking South Africa down its present course.

Historically, the SAP had been led by men (there were no

women) who'd come out of the Special Branch. As security cops, their basic orientation was to see policing as the final bulwark between apartheid order and the anarchy that must follow its demise. Their defeat during the transition was inevitable and unregretted. The same is not true of the Detective Service, however, which has suffered badly in the organisational politics of police transformation during which the commitment to prevention (translated, often, as 'proactive policing') was consciously and explicitly counterposed to a police strategy premised on reacting to crime once it had happened. As a result, detective work and detectives came to be seen as unfashionable; relics, almost, of a bygone age.

Precisely why this happened is a tale best left for another time, but its roots lie in the almost comical level of antipathy that exists between uniformed cops and the plain-clothed members of the Detective Service. To hear uniformed officers tell it, detectives are lazy, good-for-nothings who spend their days standing around braais, nursing their expanding beer bellies and talking about how to steal stuff from the evidence lockers. Detectives, by contrast, think of their uniformed colleagues as bureaucratic automatons, people who are bound up by rules and who like it that way; people who ruin the statements they take from victims and witness, and whose sole contribution at crime scenes is to stand on all the useful evidence. This mutual ill-feeling made it inevitable that after 1994, the rise to power of the uniform branch – the proactive component of the police – would mean that detective work slipped down the list of organisational priorities.

The result was the development of a vision of policing founded on the idea of crime prevention. In practice this meant the prioritisation of two interrelated approaches to reducing crime. The first was the prioritisation of visible policing: patrol work, roadblocks, cordon-and-search operations ... the kind of policing that puts uniformed men and women on the street in an effort to intimidate criminals or to catch them in the act. The second was to get the police to work with the communities they served, the relevant government departments, and do-gooders of every stripe in order to address the 'causes of crime'. Policing, understood in this way, was seen as a kind of catalyst for social re-engineering, the spark that would ignite social transformation.

Now, there has always been something quite absurd about the idea of police officers and policing acting as the fulcrum around which the re-engineering of society would turn, especially in South Africa. Policing, after all, was the coercive precondition for apartheid and its legitimacy as a tool of state power was, in 1994, woefully low. Yet, right through the 1990s, policy-makers and analysts argued that this craft, still practised by and large by the very people who had policed apartheid, would drive the transformation of South Africa's communities. This was always crazy and, thankfully, most people involved in safety and security have overcome these romantic ideas. Pretty much everyone now seems to accept that our cops do not have the inclination, training or resources to change the world. It is true that some people continue to talk about how the police could help to ensure that the local governments install street lighting or cut the grass in dangerous areas, especially when they talk about sector policing strategies, but few think that the police – rather than, oh, elected politicians, say – ought to drive the planning and implementation of community renewal strategies.

Even with these conceptual changes, even after 2000, when Jackie Selebi's more bullish reign meant that some of the woollier thinking about the role of the police in reshaping society was cast out of the organisation, the general emphasis on preventing crime remained. Though a more militarised and aggressive model of police-led crime prevention has developed, its unchanging aim has been to ensure that the police devote their energies to suppressing crime, largely through highly visible, labour-intensive operations. These are the bluntest of blunt instruments, the tactic of choice only because the organisation lacks the finesse and nuance to deal with crime in other ways. That these operations frequently net suspects in serious crimes is testimony less to the skills and intelligence applied to them than to the sheer number of offenders out there.

The detectives meanwhile have continued to receive short shrift.

★

The argument that has justified government's commitment to using its police primarily as proactive crime preventers, rather than charging them with the morally fraught business of putting people – inevitably, poor people – behind bars, draws its inspiration from a variety of sources. One is the sense, deep-rooted in most of us, that 'prevention is better than cure'. Another is the conviction that sending the poor to jail is something a post-liberation government ought not to do if it can possibly avoid it. Ultimately, though, the commitment to preventing crime has relied most heavily on a conviction that this is something policing can actually do, and that this would be the most effective and efficient use of the vast resources devoted to it. Indeed, this kind of thinking goes beyond the police: in the prisons, government's chief aim, so it says, is to reform and rehabilitate prisoners in order to prevent future crime. Similarly, the prosecution service's vision of itself has its officers doing a lot more than just prosecuting those the police arrest. Apparently, they are to use their abundant free time to help police and communities to improve their crime prevention efforts.

The instinct behind all of this is the noble conviction that institutions of the law ought to be used to straighten the crooked timber of humanity. And there would be little to complain about if there were not important negative consequences for the choices that have been made. Unfortunately, there have been, and the most important of these is that the devotion of organisational attention and resources to figuring out how to prevent crime has meant that those parts of the criminal justice system devoted to finding and punishing criminals have suffered the cruel neglect of the ugly stepchild.

The only proof one needs of this assertion, I think, is a single statistic. This is that the number of prisoners in South African jails has risen by a little more than 50% since the mid-1990s. (In fact, the prisoner population is now off its peaks of a few years ago because the rate of new admissions to our prisons seems to have fallen through the floor since 2005.) In the United Kingdom, by contrast, where the need is far less pressing, the prisoner population has grown at virtually twice the pace. In the United States, it has grown even faster, and has done so for decades.

★

The Detective Service is the most obvious example of the inadequate attention paid to the capacity of the state to find and punish offenders. This institution has never been quite as strong and smart and dedicated as its older hands claim, but there is a strong consensus in the organisation (except at the very top, where it would be impolitic to say as much) that life in a transforming Police Service has not been good to its detectives. This is the result of any number of poor policy choices, some of which seem to them to have been custom built to undermine their status. The most egregious of these was a decision, taken in 1996, to make local detectives answerable to the station commander rather than to a separate chain of command. This reversed decades of institutional, organisational and professional autonomy, and suggested, implicitly and explicitly, that detective work was subordinate to the patrol and response work done by uniformed officers. It meant that when I toured the country in 1998 talking to detectives, I found myself meeting the most profoundly miserable people imaginable: all of them thought that their organisation – their brotherhood – was collapsing around them.

Another policy decision that has had similarly negative effects in the Detective Service is the still unfinished business of 'restructuring' into oblivion most specialised investigative units and redeploying their officers to police stations. This is a process that began under earlier police management, but which has accelerated under Selebi.

These two processes are perhaps the most serious examples of the trend, but there were others. The decision, since reversed, to make detectives responsible for the running of the community service centres at police stations; the ongoing practice of requiring detectives regularly to don uniforms and conduct crime prevention operations; the establishment of the Scorpions, justified at the time by perceptions of police corruption: taken together, all have created a real sense that the investigative work done by the Detective Service is held in some contempt by senior police management. Inevitably, this has had serious consequences for morale and, because the quality of investigative work depends heavily on the self-motivation of detectives, it has had consequences for effectiveness, too. It has also made it far harder to attract and retain talented officers since most cops now have the impression that to become a detective is to take on onerous hours and, simultaneously, to reduce one's career prospects.

The upshot is that we now have too few detectives with too little experience and motivation. This helps to explain why the conviction rate for murder hovers around 20%, despite a large proportion of these crimes' having been committed by people known to the victim – crimes which should be relatively easy to solve. For robbery, a good deal fewer than 5 cases in 100 result in a conviction, a ratio that, if anything, overstates police success because so many robberies go unreported or are never entered into police databases.

The failure to build an organisationally stable, reasonably-resourced and professional Detective Service whose organisational autonomy is respected, is not just a matter of its being unable to deliver more convictions. It has also had the effect of corrupting professional ethics – never policing's strong suit in South Africa – with a disturbing number of instances having been reported in recent years in which poor cases have been buttressed with fabricated evidence. This is to say nothing of the huge concerns about corruption which is a cancer in the criminal justice system. The poisoning of a sensitive organisational ecosystem after 1994 through poor policy choices has made it far, far harder to instil new values and higher ethical and professional standards.

Nor is it just the detectives who've been neglected as institutional attention has focused on crime prevention. Prosecutors, who are among the most highly qualified and, therefore, most mobile officers in the criminal justice system, have complained for years that their salaries are uncompetitive and that their workloads are too onerous to attract the best and brightest. Instead, the National Prosecuting Authority has become a kind of finishing school for graduate lawyers unable to find places in commercial law firms, with the result that turnover rates are high and new prosecutors must be brought on stream continuously. At the same time, because the resourcing of this essential function has been neglected, prison capacity has lagged behind the growth in the population of prisoners awaiting trial or serving (ever-lengthening) sentences. The only way the prisons have managed at all is by regular 'burstings' when large numbers of prisoners are released to free up space. Failure to spend enough in order to increase prison accommodation is counter-productive in more ways than one: even if rehabilitation were a proven science (which it isn't), overcrowding has made its implementation impossible.

All of this would be a problem under any circumstances, but if there is something to the argument I have made that the post-apartheid crime wave having been driven by its own runaway internal energies, rather than underlying social and economic conditions, any decline in the state's capacity to arrest and prosecute offenders would be part of the explanation for our crime-friendly national culture. The failure to take off the streets enough people involved in crime will have made it more likely that others would join the party.

The bottom line is that South Africa does not lack for institutionalised do-goodery. It doesn't need the police to add its considerable weight to this. What we lack are institutions that draw firm legal lines in the sand and then come down heavily on people who cross those lines.

★

There is much about South Africa's detectives, prosecutors and prisons that could be improved. There are too few people in the system and many lack the skills they need. Other resources – from vehicles and crime-scene kits to official documentation and forensic specialists – are also lacking. Performance management systems, which are formidably difficult to design and prone to creating perverse incentives, are weak; all too frequently managers' commitment or competence is not what it should be. Most depressing is the realisation that a criminal justice system in a democracy is a complex set of institutions, the functioning of which depends as much on patterns of thought and behaviour that take generations to become entrenched as it does on its resources and its rules and protocols. These are not organisations that can be fixed by rolling out a new computer system or pushing staff through a two week refresher course; what has gone on in the past – both under apartheid and after it – casts a long shadow.

The most important issue of all, however, is strategic, and it revolves around reframing the purpose of the criminal justice system from 'fighting crime' to 'fighting criminals'. This means progressing from seeing the criminal justice system as one part of a wider social effort to change society, to seeing it as an institution with a singular and singularly important mission: to find and prosecute people who commit crimes. We should be trying to make it exceptionally good at doing that, rather than at healing society and smoothing out its deformations. The good thing is that much of the work is not rocket science but the dogged processing of paper and information, most of it relatively standardised. It can be done by the people we have.

What, then, would a full-blown effort to catch and prosecute violent criminals mean?

It would mean resourcing investigative and prosecutorial systems better. It would mean training, training and more training. It would mean aligning incentives in the police and prosecution services to ensure that the focus is on the kinds of crime and criminal that result in the most social harm. It would mean ensuring that officers do not focus only on the easiest of cases just to meet numerical targets.

A focus on convictions would not mean arresting everyone who ever gets into a violent altercation: the system simply cannot cope with these numbers and, in any case, arrests in these circumstances sometimes aggravate tensions between the people concerned. It would, however, mean fingerprinting them all and using our state-of-the-art digital fingerprint identification system to link as many people as possible to previous crimes, and to make available ever more prints against which to test any latent prints lifted at future crime scenes. It would mean developing a national DNA database so that blood and semen and spit left at crime scenes can be matched to suspects. A good place to start would be with the 2.5 million people the SAPS once claimed to arrest in a single year. It would mean building the finest forensic capability in the world.

Fighting criminals by pursuing arrests and convictions doesn't just mean waiting for crimes to happen and then hoping to find clues – fingerprints and DNA and witnesses – that will help identify offenders. Proactive investigations, using epidemiological techniques that identify patterns in order to identify potential suspects, are used far too seldom in South Africa. We need to raise this part of our game. We also need to build new sources of data capable of establishing links between crimes and criminals. Given the role of prisons in developing criminal networks, it is a pity, for instance, that we have no database that can trace who has shared prison cells with whom over the past ten years. We should be tapping every data source we have, from financial transactions to cellphone records, to identify suspects. Since the crimes we fear are largely vehicle-borne and most people carry cellphones, we should be making all our cellphones and cars trackable in real time.

Tackling violent criminals head on would not mean lengthening already punitive sentences. Counter-intuitive as it may seem, it makes more sense to send larger numbers of violent people to jail for shorter periods, than to imprison smaller numbers for longer: prison space is a scarce resource and it must be husbanded. Nor does it mean that the rights of prisoners to be treated humanely should be neglected: it's hard enough for people to come out of prison no worse than when they entered without allowing conditions to deteriorate further. It does mean, however, that more prison space should be built and built quickly, and the Department of Correctional Service's inability to roll out either new prisons or electronic monitoring systems should be a national scandal.

A more aggressive approach to criminals would mean making the unauthorised carrying of a firearm a priority offence while also working hard to restrict access to guns. It would involve tasking detectives to work backwards from every gun crime to the source of the weapon so that anyone who has lost a firearm negligently can be held financially liable for whatever harm it causes later. Anyone who sold the last drink to an obviously intoxicated patron who subsequently committed some or other outrage, should be named, shamed and sued. Similarly, we should come down hard on anyone who helps a criminal make use of the proceeds of crime, as well as on the car dealers and estate agents and anyone else who doesn't alert the authorities to customers with funds they should be suspicious about. A few well-chosen examples might make a big difference.

Institutionally, developing our capacity to solve cases means recognising that detective work is different from the work done by uniformed police officers, and allowing organisational structures in the police, and individual career paths, to reflect that. Of course, detectives should talk to and work with their uniformed counterparts, and they should have the same priorities. But detectives ought to work as closely with local prosecutors as they do with the local uniforms and should, therefore, have the space to manage this relationship themselves. While the establishment of specialised detective units has its dangers, the present approach, which assumes that these are almost never the right answer to any question, is wrong: done wisely, specialisation can make police investigations much more nimble. It is also essential for managing talent in the Police Service, especially because it is so large and unwieldy.

I have much less to say about the courts and prisons, save that poor prosecutions can ruin perfectly well-investigated cases. So, too, can delays in court because witnesses forget, die or simply lose interest. It is imperative, therefore, that the capacity of courts grows at least as quickly as the capacity of the detectives: that means more magistrates, prosecutors and translators. Getting courts to sit more hours per day has proved to be difficult, so perhaps it is time to bite the bullet and resource the system so that many more courts are sitting.

Finally, our overcrowded prisons will rehabilitate no-one. They are also a potential time bomb that needs to be defused. We need to build more prison space, and do it more cheaply than present methods allow.

★

It is important not to overstate the impact that the problems in the criminal justice system have had on the rise in crime in South Africa. Nor should one oversell the effect that a reversal of this would have today. A plausible case might even be made that, given the volume of crime that our criminal justice system must process, our conviction rates are not all that bad. By way of comparison, it may well be that the British police achieve convictions in more than half of all murders, but then they have only 800 cases a year. We have a similar number of police officers, but twenty times as many murders. Besides, depending on what assumptions one makes about the extent to which a crime like robbery is undercounted by police statistics, you could argue that if our conviction rate is something like 3%, then someone committing 30 crimes a year – a not unattainable number for an ambitious mugger – would stand a pretty good chance of being caught for at least one of them. It may not be high enough, but the risk of being caught and convicted is not negligible.

The crucial point, though, is that despite ranking in the top five places in the world in terms of per capita prisoner numbers, the face-slappingly obvious fact is that too few of our worst offenders are behind bars: when we look at countries' prisoner populations in relation to the number of murders committed from a global perspective, South Africa ranks towards the very bottom of the list.

The fact that too few criminals are behind bars means that those on the streets and in our communities continue to commit their crimes and, perhaps more importantly, continue to create a social context in which other people are making similar choices. We need, therefore, to put many more violent offenders away. But what kind of numbers would we be talking about?

One approach – the wrong one – would be to say that we need jail space for everyone who commits a serious crime. This may be desirable from one point of view, but it would be hopelessly unaffordable and, more to the point, utterly unachievable. A back-of-the-envelope guesstimate is that there must have been between 250 000 and 500 000 people involved in just the murders, rapes and armed robberies committed in 2006/07. To get to this number I sucked from my thumb assumptions about the degree of under-reporting of rape and armed robbery, as well as for the average number of offenders involved in each crime. I also tried to make allowance for the fact that the typical offender would commit more than one crime (and more than one type of crime) in the course of the year. Even so, my calculation means that between 2.5 and 4 per cent of men between the ages of 15 and 50, or between 1 man in 40 and 1 man in 25, committed at least one murder, rape or armed robbery in 2006/07. That is a substantial proportion of the population, especially if we consider that serious crimes like assault, attempted murder, car theft and burglary haven't been included in the estimate.

It is impossible to imagine building sufficient prisons to accommodate as many as half-a-million new occupants, especially since our prisoner population, though off its peaks, at 162 000, is already very large by international standards. Still, in a country with a crime problem like ours, it doesn't seem unreasonable to think that doubling the number of convicted prisoners in eight or ten years would be beyond the pale. This is something the United States did twice in recent years – first between 1980 and 1989 and then again between 1990 and 2002, with numbers continuing to grow after that, too. In all, by the end of the 20th century there were four times as many prisoners in American jails and prisons than there'd been 25 years before. The role that increased imprisonment played in reducing crime in America is much debated by academics, policy-makers and activists, but I cannot see how it could not have been an important factor, even if it has scarred that society in many other ways. In comparison with this, the 50% rise in prisoner numbers in South Africa since 1994 is hopelessly modest.

There are good reasons for a white writer, a member of the middle classes, to be humble when advocating a policy change that would lead to significantly larger numbers of poor black men going to jail: prison is an unrelievedly awful institution, and governments that lock up large proportions of their citizenry seldom make their societies better places to live. This is certainly true of the world's more authoritarian societies, but even in America, a growing body of evidence suggests that the rapid growth of prisoner numbers has deepened the poverty of the underclass and fuelled inequality.

Increasing our conviction rates is not going to be easy and, even if achieved, may not make as big a difference to crime levels as some might hope: if criminality is as entrenched as some fear, then there may not be any interventions that will bring it down in the short term. Still, increased conviction rates would necessarily have to lead to fewer criminals on the street, surely something that would make crime prevention activities that much more successful.

More importantly, perhaps, by making crime demonstrably a bad choice, this is the one intervention that has a chance of changing the cultural tone. This is especially true if we were to focus attention on crimes of violence. If we did that, not only would we be putting behind bars people who deserve to be in prison and whose removal from our communities would mean they could no longer commit crimes there, not only would we be changing the risk–reward calculation, but we would also be setting much more clearly defined boundaries around what kind of behaviour is and is not acceptable.

This could be hugely significant.

In an earlier chapter, I suggested that our crime wave might be understood by analogy to a party: as the dance floor fills up, more and more people, some of them shy and awkward, come off the walls to join in. The same, I think, is true of crime. As more and more people engage in criminality, its sheer prevalence drags in others, many of whom would not get involved if fewer people were not already doing it. At my most optimistic, I think that an aggressive programme aimed at incarcerating substantially larger numbers of violent offenders would be a bit like a bouncer wading onto the dance floor and throwing some of the more exuberant guests out of the building.

This approach to South Africa's crime problem might have a far greater impact than would be predicted if one thinks only of the effects incarceration has on incapacitating those who are behind bars from committing more crimes and deterring some others for whom the jailed serve as an object lesson. Perhaps it could change the whole cultural context within which criminals and potential criminals weigh up their options. Done well, it might go some way towards killing the party, as people progressively choose to return to their tables rather than dance in increasingly empty spaces.

None of which means that putting on music with a less wild and crazy beat would not be a good idea, too. To do that, though, quite a lot needs to be done to build and rebuild the half-made structures of our society.

CHAPTER NINE

IT'S ABOUT VALUES, STUPID!

If you dislike formulaic answers to important questions, reading most accounts of what could be done to make South Africa less criminogenic can be a little depressing. All the usual suspects appear: our streets would be safer if more people were richer and better educated; we would sleep better at night if inequalities were blunted and if young men had more hope of getting decent jobs; there'd be less thuggery in the future if today's children suffered less abuse, witnessed less violence, or were offered more reason for hope.

No moderately sensitive or sensible South African would need much help to draft a similar list and, for that reason, I am not going to spend much time here repeating the obvious. Save to say that all of it is true. Getting these things right would make a huge difference. The point about the analysis I have offered up to this point, however, is that the unexamined middle, the transmission mechanism between our poor economic indicators and our dreadful crime problem, is a social climate that aggravates rather than ameliorates the tendency to violence. This, I believe, is itself an effect of the high levels of crime we already have. Dealing more decisively with criminals will change this, but there is a good deal more that might be done, too.

Banal as it sounds, the key question is one of values.

*

Government has long recognised that some of the values held by South Africans are among the many causes of crime. Whether it is termed 'public values and education' (as it was in the NCPS) or the Moral Regeneration Movement, this insight has resulted in proposals, at least, for dedicated government programmes aimed at teaching South Africans to be less tolerant of crime. Thus, to the question, 'What makes people good?' — a question that is central, in one way or another, to the unsatisfied wrestlings of every philosopher since Aristotle — we are offered a disarmingly simple answer: people are to be made good through better education.

Precisely who ought to be doing this educating varies. Sometimes the articulation of this seems to imply the self-regarding idea that politicians and other celebrities should be our role models, something that might encourage the less cautious among us to suggest that these would-be physicians heal themselves first. Sometimes, the teaching of morality is to be left to the churches (and, sometimes, other components of civil society). But, most of the time, government seems to have the schools in mind as its drivers of a sound moral education.

There are important problems with this, not the least of which is that our schools may not be all that good at teaching, much less teaching morality. This was demonstrated by an open letter to primary school principals from one of their bosses, a deputy director-general of the Department of Education, dated as recently as 14 August 2006. Still available, helpfully, on the department's website, it has as its ingenuous title, 'Let's teach our children to read!' Its second paragraph is the only evidence anyone will ever need for doubting the capacity of our schools to offer a moral education: 'Since the introduction of the National Curriculum Statement', it says, referring to Outcomes-Based Education, 'many teachers believe they do not have to teach reading any more. Nothing,' it assures them, 'could be further from the truth.'

Primary school teachers who need reminding that they ought to be teaching children to read, are not, I would submit, fully equipped to teach morality.

Except that they are already teaching a morality of a kind.

Moral behaviour is not something that is learnt by rote. It is, I think, much more like a set of habits – of honesty and judgement and discipline and duty – that are formed by observing others and by responding to rewards and punishments. If this is right, then schools in which teachers do not teach reading, even though the Education Department thinks it is 'probably' the most essential skill to be taught, are teaching the morality of absenteeism and missed classes, of unfinished curricula and unpredictable consequences.

Teachers are not alone in this, of course. Officials at the Department of Home Affairs, who deprive a grandmother of her right to a pension when they fail to issue her ID book, but who will happily accept a bribe to provide an immigrant with false papers, teach lessons in morality. So, too, do police officers who respond lethargically to calls for assistance, and their bosses when they imply that the rise in violent crime is a figment of our collective imagination. The same is true of traffic cops who would rather a speeding driver bought them lunch than issue a ticket, and nurses whose patients develop bedsores or who abandon pregnant women to give birth alone. Politicians, whose personal commitment to truth-telling is often more than a little suspect, who defend instinctively their officials when wrong-doing is identified, and who hang out with the likes of the late Brett Kebble, also send out messages about what kind of behaviour is acceptable.

Nor is our business community – recently rated as among the most likely to pay bribes in African countries – always offering object lessons in good behaviour. And it is not just bribe-paying and the greedy ethos of conspicuous consumption that convey bad ideas about morality: retailers who make much of their money by extending expensive loans to people who can't afford them have made a virtue out of taking people to the cleaners.

Obviously, most people do better than the caricatures offered here. Obviously, also, these problems exist to a greater or lesser extent everywhere: George W Bush and his cronies, to cite a non-random example, are no more honest than even the most self-serving South African politician, and are often a good deal worse. The difference between South Africa and the United States, however, is that the DNA of our the major institutions has been shaped by the cynicism and arbitrariness of apartheid, so there is little experience of a different logic on which state institutions should rely. This matters because the moral climate created by our institutions is a function not just of what they deliver and at what cost, but of how they conduct themselves. In this, as in so much else, South Africans' experience of our institutions and the ethics of their work depends on whom one is. If you're rich, most of the institutions with which you deal make rational, predictable, reasonably honest decisions and, if they do not, there is always the possibility of laying a complaint or taking your business elsewhere. If you're poor, on the other hand, your world is governed by the impenetrable logic of failed and failing schools, inaccessible and self-dealing public officials, and the Mafia-ethics of the taxi industry. There is no-one to complain to and no competition. Reason and self-discipline are the exception in this world, and the lessons learnt from your experience of the world are, therefore, quite different from those learnt by those whose experience is of reasoned, rational institutions.

Because the sources of inappropriate moral lessons are multiple and various, it is enormously difficult to mount a successful campaign of deliberate moral re-education. Certainly, the 'Don't do crime' campaigns launched in the late 1990s were a spectacular waste of effort. Part of the problem, though, is that moral regeneration campaigns, which start with the assumption that teaching moral behaviour is merely a matter of getting bums on the seats of churches or schools, badly misconstrue the manner in which values are learnt. They assume that morality is taught didactically, as one might teach a recipe or the multiplication tables, rather than learnt through the experience of the behaviour of people and institutions around us.

One reason the if-you-teach-them-they'll-be-good school

of behaviour modification has come to dominate policy thinking on this may be that many of our policy-makers began their public lives as believers in one or another version of Marxism. This is a doctrine that holds that moral prescripts have no independent validity. Instead, they are deemed to come from, and reflect, the ruling ideology, one that works primarily to obscure the injustices of the social order. This is not a helpful premise if one is seeking to understand how behaviour might be shaped by changes in moral sentiment, or how to effect those changes. But, if values are not learnt like this and emerge, instead, from the lessons people draw from their experience of the world around them, the institution-building tasks that we confront are both more difficult and more subtle than has generally been recognised.

Institutions that act rationally, that treat people fairly, that do what they say they'll do, and engage the world honestly, generate different social effects than those whose actions are arbitrary, whose officials are manifestly self-interested or dishonest, and which consistently fail to do their duty. The style of the former demonstrates that honesty and diligence and application matter; the style of the latter demonstrates the opposite. Delivery is important, to be sure. But so too is the manner in which institutions act and the way they speak.

One priority, then, that government could set itself in changing the country's moral climate is to ensure that public institutions express and reflect sound values. This must manifest in more than just their commitment to delivering goods and services to the poor and in the rhetoric of their vision statements; it must be reflected in their treating citizens as adults and in conducting themselves with integrity and dignity.

Creating a society based on the dignity of every individual is not just about building more houses, cleaning the streets more often or making the Springbok rugby team more representative. It is also about behaving in a way that takes seriously the behavioural niceties, the courtesies and conventions, that are sometimes assumed by the way the Constitution frames public administration but which are often trampled on in practice.

Tautological it may be, but if we want people to behave more decently, we need to become a more decent society.

*

If the implication of the previous section is that it would help the fight against crime if everyone tried to be just a little nicer, it would be dishonest not to acknowledge that this piece of policy advice is fantastically impractical. In all likelihood, it would also not make much difference to crime levels all that quickly. There is, however, another problem, a dilemma that may well be unresolvable. Certainly, I cannot resolve it. This is that many of the actions individual South Africans take – that they are forced to take – to increase their safety, often have the effect of pushing people further apart from one another. This would be bad enough if the pushing away were an unintended consequence of their individual actions. In fact, that is their precise purpose.

Examples of what I mean abound. Think about boomgates in the suburbs, which work largely to the extent that they limit the flow of strangers through the area. Think about the cops who stop young, black men in the streets of predominantly white areas. Think about the way we modify our travel patterns so as to avoid areas where we are afraid to stop. Think about the suspicion with which we greet strangers and our unwillingness to help anyone we do not know. The list is endless and, in a country with our history, these actions reinforce the patterns of social interaction that arose under apartheid.

Nor is it just our security measures that drive wedges between people. Crime does that pretty efficiently all by itself. Every time someone is mugged or hijacked, every time voices in the street rise in anger and fists fly, every time we read of a child's trauma at the loss of her father, each of us huddles down a little closer to our families. In the process, bonds that might otherwise link us in webs of mutual knowledge and trust are weakened. Within our communities, it encourages people to look to their own and to fear others, to form gangs of vigilantes to terrorise people who live in the area and don't have the decency to commit their crimes elsewhere.

Crime reinforces some of our grosser patterns of social interaction while tearing apart other bonds that need strengthening. At the same time, it makes the forging of new bonds harder. It leaves one thinking, sometimes, that there is little between us save for anger and hostility and suspicion and mutual misunderstanding.

All of which is a disaster for any programme aimed at making South Africa a nicer, more decent place to live.

There are two possible responses to this problem. The first is to say that, however strongly individuals might feel about increasing their personal security, as a nation, we must follow a path down which we will, in the end, emerge as a better, nicer people. Instead of building moats, we could choose to build bridges. This, roughly speaking, is the instinct of those who offer principled objections to the idea of booming off our suburbs.

The second response to the bridges–or–moats dilemma is to say that physical security trumps all other priorities. If, in the course of building up our walls, we make the forging of a more decent society harder, then that is a price we just have to pay. This is the instinct of those who fear the consequences of building low–income housing in middle– and upper–income suburbs.

The bitch of it is that squaring this circle may be impossible. The twin imperatives – to do what we can to increase personal security and to do what we can to forge better social bonds – flow in diametrically opposed directions; they cannot be reconciled.

I have no idea how we get out of this dilemma. Or even if we can.

★

Apart from the abstractions involved in building a more decent society, there are other interventions which might be made to impact on how much crime is committed. The most important of these revolves around the form of our cities, the human settlements in which most of our crime is committed. The most obvious examples of the challenges come from the country's informal settlements.

The warrens of shacks that have mushroomed around

some of the major urban townships, with their one- or two-roomed homes, dwellings that freeze in winter, broil in summer and leak in the rain, must be unspeakably horrible places to live. Their only merit is their proximity to areas in which work may be found or where subsistence commerce is possible. Millions of South Africans live by their wits in these slums, cut off from the economy, the law and each other. From a policing point of view, settlements like these are a black hole: patrol work is dangerous where it isn't physically impossible; cops can seldom enter these areas without their suspects being alerted; and, when they do, the lack of street names and house numbers makes finding victims and witnesses time-consuming and difficult. All of which would matter much less if these spaces didn't foster the kinds of tensions that explode into murderous rage, if they were not places where many people are so poor that they must sometimes resort to crime just to put food on the table, and if homes of tin and cardboard were not so enormously difficult to secure.

Careful, vigorous urban redevelopment in these areas could make a big difference to crime.

The problem with informal settlements, though, is not just that they create the potential for crime in the here and now, but that this environment makes raising healthy families extremely difficult. In this, our shack settlements are but one example of the many ways in which the structure of our society makes a healthy family life harder to achieve. There are, for instance, something approaching a million domestic workers in South Africa, a substantial proportion of whom spend most of their time apart from their children. There are also hundreds of thousands of men in hostels on mines and in townships near industrial areas. Many see their wives and kids irregularly, leaving their children to grow up without fathers. In fact, if researchers from the Human Sciences Research Council are to be believed, a good deal more than a third of children in some communities are born to parents who are not married.

These things matter, not because growing up in the squalid conditions of an informal settlement or on the emotional fault-lines of broken homes means that one must inevitably turn to crime, but because it is not unreasonable to think that, on average, these kinds of conditions are likely to produce people with lower resilience to the temptations of criminality, people who will be that much more likely to turn to crime if the context is remotely conducive. This, I think, must be especially true of overcrowded living conditions where it is hard to believe that growing children could develop a sense of the inviolability of their own bodies, much less of the bodies of those around them.

Generally, one should be suspicious of any government's intrusions into family life. Well-intended though they may be, bureaucrats and politicians seldom know better what is good for a family than do its members. Happily, public policy since 1994 has almost certainly helped to reduce the dysfunctionality of our family life: government has built houses (small and crowded though they are, they are better than shacks); it has pursued economic policies that have begun to create jobs; it has thrown money into erecting a social safety net around children and the elderly. The one gaping hole in all of this is HIV/AIDS, the neglect of which has robbed hundreds of thousands of children of one or both parents, and has undermined much of the good that has been done elsewhere. Stigmatising orphans should be avoided, but child-headed households are not exactly conducive to producing model citizens.

The prevention of crime should be the last reason why a government would commit itself to family-friendly policies, and there is something particularly offensive about the notion that crime should be the reason for tackling an epidemic that has caused as much misery as has AIDS. Still, for what it is worth, rolling out AIDS prevention and treatment aggressively would almost certainly help make future generations of South Africans safer than they are going to be otherwise. In the absence of alternatives that will save more young parents' lives, we should be investing like mad in social work services.

*

If developing better social values and becoming nicer to one another should be one element of how we develop a society in which people choose not to do crime, and if helping to foster more functional families is another, a third is making sure that the economy grows and that as many people as possible share in the benefits of this.

In this, I am more optimistic than many people because I cannot see how our growing safety net cannot but have helped improve life at the bottom of our social order. We have a great many poor people and the distribution of income is far from satisfactory, but there is probably no other country on the planet where nearly a quarter of all citizens receive a social grant of some kind or another. From the point of view both of one's pocket and one's soul, receiving a modest grant is nowhere near as good as receiving a decent salary. But it is also better than the only realistic alternative – receiving nothing.

If I am right about our crime problems having cultural rather than economic roots, the key challenges are not so much about growing the economy as they are about changing the way in which economic, social and political processes leave so many excluded. Because of the structural inequalities in almost every sphere, a large proportion of people live in social spaces over which they have so little control one might think of them as driftwood. This lack of control over one's life must inevitably mean that the basic idea that one can take responsibility for oneself will find no purchase. If you are forever treated as the victim of circumstances – if you *are* forever the victim of circumstances – how on earth do you develop a sense that your destiny is something you can choose? And, if you do not see yourself and your world in these terms, is it reasonable to expect responsible choices, choices that take account of the future and of other people's rights and interests? You cannot simply instruct people to behave more responsibly. If people are to behave responsibly, they must have control over their lives. The latter is a precondition of the former.

The point is that our values are learnt through the circumstances and experiences of our lives. These seldom produce people with the unconditional values of the saints. But the better, the more stable, and the more reasoned the world in which we live, the more likely it is that people will have higher thresholds – of want and of social acceptability –

before engaging in crime. While we need to change the context by putting larger numbers of offenders behind bars, we also need to remake those parts of our world which destabilise and devalue ordinary lives and which, in the process, reduce resilience to the lure of crime.

CHAPTER TEN
HOPE OR DESPAIR?

In a country with a long list of urgent problems, crime is one of the most pressing. The direct pain and trauma it causes, the fear and despair it engenders, the social and political distortions it creates and reinforces: there are any number of reasons why crime is as high up on the national agenda as it is. The trouble is that it has been high on the agenda for a long while now, and the pace at which levels of safety are improving – if they are improving – is far, far too slow. For many with the means, the consequence of this is that the question of uprooting themselves and their families and settling elsewhere, with all the difficulties that entails, nags away at them, adding its own miseries to daily life. For those without the means to contemplate emigration, other crime-related anxieties more than compensate. What, then, is the prognosis? Are things going to improve or deteriorate? Should we feel hope or despair?

As with all the other questions posed in this book, this one admits of no unambiguous, unqualified answers, and it is almost impossible to list, much less weigh, all the various factors that might decide the issue. What follows is a discussion of the impact that will be made by the four variables I think will turn out to be most important: economic growth, demographic change, the performance of the criminal justice system, and technological innovation.

★

By far the most decisive factor in determining whether levels of safety will improve or deteriorate in the foreseeable future is the economy.

The importance I'm attaching to the economy may sound odd given the emphasis I placed earlier on non-economic factors in explaining the crime wave. But it is justified because a growing economy does not just create jobs and reduce the material causes of crime: the state's having the resources to build a better criminal justice system and erect a more tightly woven safety net around the poor and vulnerable is a precondition for improving levels of safety.

But there is another, more disturbing reason for thinking that economic growth is a prerequisite for reduced criminality: the violent reaction of far too many people when a tremor runs through their finances. Consider, for example, how quickly the private security industry strike in the first quarter of 2006 turned violent. Workers, living a hand-to-mouth existence and made suddenly more insecure financially than they had been by the no-work-no-pay rule, very quickly turned to extreme violence to enforce the strike. Well over 50 people, most but not all of them deemed 'scabs', were killed. Later, in 2007, when public service workers went on strike, they too showed a disturbing propensity to turn to violence, with teachers, in some cases, reported to have shot at, or strangled, learners coming to school to write mid-year exams.

The security strike of 2006 also coincided with a sudden spike in crime in South Africa, one which lasted into the months after the strike. This, I think, was less the effect of there being fewer security guards working our streets and businesses, than it was of the security guards themselves turning to crime to put bread on the table and pressure on their employers. That the surge in crime lasted beyond the strike may have been because of the copycat effect I have described earlier, or of the fact that striking workers took out extortionately-priced loans while not earning their salaries, incurring debts they had to service over the following months.

The financial lives of lowly paid workers are extraordinary in their precariousness, but if this is how financially vulnerable workers respond to the increased stress put on their wallets by a short, if traumatic strike, any coughing of the economic engine that threw thousands of people out of work, might have devastating consequences for levels of violence. It would be too strong to say that the rapid economic growth of recent years has papered over some of the cracks in our society, but it may be that growth needs to persist a good deal longer before a wide enough margin of safety is built into the lives of ordinary people. Until that happens, the consequences of a serious economic slow-down may be too horrible to contemplate.

★

If economic growth is vital because increased financial stress might be seriously destabilising, its importance increases because the state is going to need a lot of resources to deal with the demographic changes that continue to transform our society.

The age structure of South African society is notoriously unbalanced. We are a very young society: the average South African is only 27 years old and half our population is under the age of 24. The most serious issue is that age-group cohorts below the age of 18 are larger today than they have ever been, a phenomenon that makes it harder for already floundering social institutions to produce and reproduce sound civic values.

This would be hard enough if it were not also the case that soon, more and more young people will have grown up in households that have been devastated by AIDS. A not insignificant proportion will have lost one or both parents, many more will have come from families that, at a minimum, would have had to stretch their resources to help their struggling relatives.

It is unfortunate that this kind of discussion runs the real risk of adding to the stigma that attaches to AIDS and AIDS-orphanhood. Nevertheless, it would be irresponsible for a government to assume that as destabilising an epidemic as AIDS would not have very serious consequences for the way in which families bring up their children. We need, therefore, to invest large chunks of the income flowing from our growing economy into stabilising the South African family. This needs to be in the form of housing and social services, but, by far the most important intervention would be the rapid rollout of AIDS treatment since this will keep sick parents alive longer.

Managed well, the maturation of large cohorts of young people need not result in ever-growing levels of crime. But if this is to happen, we need to invest vast resources in making sure that children live lives that are as free of these kinds of shock as possible, and that when shocks are unavoidable, the effect is mitigated.

If cohorts of young people and the effects of AIDS are two key demographic variables which may affect crime levels, a third is the wild card of Zimbabwe and other Zimbabwe-like meltdowns in the region.

Foreigners, to repeat a point made earlier, are not the source of South Africa's crime problems. But living in a rough neighbourhood does affect the outlook for criminality: gangs of angry and unpaid soldiers and former soldiers just across the border would be bad for South African crime rates; so too would be refugee camps, which are everywhere in the world a source of destabilisation. I tend to think that reports of there being 2 million or more Zimbabweans in South Africa are exaggerated, if only because there are only 13 million Zimbabweans in the whole world. Besides, at the time of writing, all the violence and horror in Iraq had generated only a little more than 2 million refugees from a population twice as large as Zimbabwe's. Whatever the true number, were hundreds of thousands of new economic and political refugees to stream across the Limpopo, the pressure on our cities and government departments, the tensions that would emerge in our society, will make the resort to crime that much more likely for both South Africans and newly arrived Zimbabweans.

★

If, from the point of view of levels of crime, the potential downside of an economic slump is pretty awful, and if other demographic changes may not be benign, there are two bright spots on the horizon: the workings of the criminal justice system and technological innovation.

To regard the criminal justice system as a reason for hope is not, I imagine, the most common of responses. As I have argued throughout the book, policing and law enforcement have not done anywhere near as much as they might have to roll back the crime wave. Indeed, poor decisions made about criminal justice over the past fifteen years or so have made things worse. But that is precisely why this is a reason for hope, for imagine how we'd feel if we had the levels of crime we do but our police and courts and prisons were operating much more effectively than they are? It would be at that point that despair would be completely justified. As it stands, however, focusing on the business of catching, convicting and incarcerating the bad guys, and pumping resources into the system could, I believe, create a virtuous circle of the reduction in crime leading to a changing social context within which potential criminals would be making their choices. This issue was discussed at some length earlier, and need not be repeated here.

The last factor that will shape crime in the future is technology, and, in some ways, it may be the most decisive.

*

Technological advances will affect crime in a number of different ways by changing the patterns of opportunity and reward that criminals must negotiate, as well as by improving the capacity of the state to find and prosecute them effectively. It is likely, for instance, that in the not-too-distant future, top-end cars will be unstealable. Ignition systems will rely on biometric readings of voice prints or iris scans; major parts will all be 'smart' and will work only with parts whose electronic signatures they recognise; the power to 'blacklist' stolen vehicles in much the same way as is now done with stolen cellphones, will be a standard feature. Like car security, home security will become ever more sophisticated and effective.

For a price, then, the middle classes will be relatively safe in their cars and their homes. Work, too, will become safer as the formal economy becomes increasingly cashless in its functioning, with credit, debit and smart cards, as well as cellphone and internet banking, all reducing the amount of cash in circulation.

Both increased security and the trend to cashless-ness in the formal economy will change the pattern of crime. In some cases, extraordinarily audacious and vicious criminals will try to find ways to overcome these defences using increased violence. For the most part, however, motivated offenders will have to find other kinds of targets. And that means that there will be some displacement of criminal energy to those parts of the economy that cannot do without cash, and to people who cannot afford the most effective forms of security.

Less ambiguous – in relation to crime, if not to the right to privacy – could be the way new technologies might be used to identify, track and convict offenders. Whether it is DNA databases or the real-time tracking of cars and cellphones, it may be that we will live in a society that is less free, but in which it will be exceptionally hard to get away with some crimes. It may even be that new forms of electronic tagging will mean that some of the expenses associated with prison-building will be avoided: if it is possible to monitor continuously the movements of people convicted of crimes in ways that they cannot overcome, it would also be possible to hold even serious offenders in much less secure facilities than we do now. That might mean that a cheap barbed-wire fence around a disused school would turn it into a secure prison, radically reducing one of the most serious constraints on implementing a more aggressive approach to law enforcement: the sheer cost of doing so.

The great thing about technological advance is that, while maximising the impact of some technologies will require boldness in government's decision-making, in most cases the market will generate these offerings all by itself. Technology-based improvements in safety are unstoppable and irreversible. They will not end crime in South Africa, but their contribution could make a huge difference to levels of safety, especially for those who can afford the very best.

★

In the best-case scenario, then, sustained economic growth that creates jobs would address some of the material causes of crime. It would also fill state coffers with the funds it needs to build a better, more incarceration-focused criminal justice system, as well as erect more tightly woven safety nets. Both of these would be important because demographic changes – the youth bomb that is still filtering through the age structure of the population, the devastation of families as a result of AIDS, and the potential that we will receive waves of refugees from north of the border – may put even more pressure on our social system. Add to this rapid technological change which would improve personal security and make for more effective investigative work, and there is every reason to hope that crime levels will improve.

By the same token, of course, there is no guarantee that these dynamics will set in: an economic slump, and all bets would be off. The argument of this book, however, has been that a chain reaction set in at some point in the past few decades, which has seen develop a self-reinforcing cycle in which high levels of crime have created a context that favours their perpetuation. To overcome this, many things need to be put in place, and economic growth will be a necessary, but not sufficient, condition for turning the tide. Apart from growth, the single most important condition for getting crime right is that we plan our policies on the premise that a high-crime society must also be a high-incarceration society.

This is not a comfortable thing for someone who considers himself a liberal – in an old fashioned way – to say. Prisons are awful, awful institutions and they do no-one who passes their gates any good. They are, to paraphrase Churchill, the worst solution to a society's crime problem, except for all the others that have been tried. This is the bullet that government, however well-intentioned its desire to uplift rather than punish, will simply have to bite. What may be at stake is not just the safety of its citizens, but the safety of democracy itself. This is because one of the risks that exceptionally high levels of crime create is that at some point in the future, a large constituency will exist for some truly dreadful responses to the lack of public safety.

We have, I believe, no reason to think ourselves immune from the kind of popular authoritarianism that has arisen in societies across the developing world when people – especially in the middle classes – feel their way of life to be threatened. There is at least some evidence of this already: after the first colloquium between business and government on crime, an event that led to the creation of the much more establishment-minded Business Against Crime, a resolution was adopted that called for the suspension of the right to bail and various other measures that would have curtailed constitutional rights. These calls are not made by responsible people today, but that reserve will not last forever. Indeed, even in America, the right to a fair trial is under greater threat today than it has been for generations.

At the moment, of course, there is no prospect of a renunciation of our liberal-democratic constitutional order: the ANC, which is the natural party of government, is wedded to a vision of itself as a modern, liberal party of social democracy. But, as Bill Clinton and Tony Blair have proved, the programme of a political party is only partly a result of its traditions; new agendas can quickly gain ground. It is not impossible to imagine circumstances in which popular anger about crime and the sometimes illiberal instincts of the middle classes will combine to bring to office a leadership altogether less

179

sympathetic to the rights a liberal democracy guarantees its citizenry.

Anyone who doubts that these are real risks needs to ask themselves only one question: if they were to come to power and were under serious pressure to do something about a crime wave, what would be the instinctive responses of some of the present leadership of the ANC Youth League?

★

If the analysis presented in this book is not overly optimistic, it is the result of my conviction that our crime problems, like many of the other challenges we face, are a result of our living in a society that one might call, using a phrase of VS Naipaul's, 'half-made'.

We have emerged, it is true, from the oppressions and cruelties of colonialism and apartheid, but we could conceivably retreat into the disorder that has characterised other post-colonial societies. The idea that we are a half-made society is related to, but different from, the more frequently used notion of our being a 'society in transition'. It is a less optimistic phrase because a process of transition, with its latent imagery of movement, seems to imply that we are heading towards some clearly defined end-state.

If we are to build the country we clearly have the potential to be, if we are to transcend our half-completedness, it is absolutely essential that we build a state that can protect its citizens from the more dangerous of their compatriots. To the extent that the analysis I've offered does not assume we will overcome our problems, it may be because, while our language makes nonsensical the idea that a society could be in transition forever, something that is half-made could remain that way until the end of time.

REFERENCES

(The numbers on the left below indicate the page number in the text)

33   The formula that South Africa's problem is not the volume of crime but its violence comes from Chris Stone, 2006, *Crime, justice, and growth in South Africa: Toward a plausible contribution from criminal justice to economic growth*, CID Working Papers 131, Centre for International Development, Harvard, p4.

37   and elsewhere. The international crime statistics that appear in this book come from numerous sources including Interpol, the United Nations Office on Drugs and Crime, the United Nations Development Programme and the World Health Organisation. The statistics in these sources seldom correspond with each other exactly, but all will be available at www.antonyaltbeker.com.

38   On the failings of international crime stats, see Altbeker, 2005, 'Puzzling statistics' in *SA Crime Quarterly* 11, Institute for Security Studies, Pretoria, pp1–8.

38   On the problem of divergent definitions of crime and variations in reporting rates, see Newman and Howard, 1999, 'Data sources and their use' in Newman (ed), *Global Report on Crime and Justice*, United Nations Office on Drugs and Crime, Oxford University Press, Oxford, pp1–25.

38   'in Jordan … with legal impunity': Amos Elon, 2003, 'An unsentimental education' in *New York Review of Books* Vol. 50, No. 9.

44 'Stanford and Rhodes': see my paper prepared for, but not yet published by, the MRC, 'Murder and Robbery: A tale of two trends'.

46 Victimisation survey results were helpfully summarised in UNDP, 2004, *Human Development Report 2004: Cultural Liberty in Today's Diverse World*, United Nations Development Programme, New York, pp215-6.

47 'people between ... twice the adult rate': Leoschut and Burton, 2005, *How rich the Rewards? Results of the 2005 National Youth Victimisation Study*, Centre for Justice and Crime Prevention, Cape Town.

47 Statistics on the proportion of robberies committed with a firearm come from Anna Alvazzi del Frate & John van Kesteren, 2004, 'The ICVS in the Developing World', *International Journal of Comparative Criminology* 2(1), De Sitter Publications, pp57-76.

48 'the distinctive ... its violence': see note to p19.

49 All South African crime statistics are from the SAPS and are available at www.saps.gov.za

50 'There are many people ... to the authorities': Ted Leggett, 2002, 'Improved crime reporting: Is South Africa's crime wave a statistical illusion?', *SA Crime Quarterly*, No. 1, Institute for Security Studies, Pretoria.

51 'victimisation survey completed in 2003': Burton, Du Plessis, Leggett, Louw, Mistry and Van Vuuren, 2004, *National Victims of Crime Survey: South Africa 2003*, Institute for Security Studies, Pretoria, p107.

52 'even in North America': Alvazzi del Frate and Van Kesteren, *op cit*.

53 'as 80% of murders fall in this category': SAPS Annual Report, 2005/06; Interview with Charles Nqakula, 'Bringing it home', *Financial Mail*, 6 April 2007.

53 'I have argued elsewhere': Altbeker, 'Building on a shaking premise' in *The Weekender* of 28 April 2007.

62 'In 2001 ... were white': Richard Matzpolous (ed), 2002, *A Profile of Fatal Injuries in South Africa: 2001*, Medical Research Council, Cape Town, p17.

63 'as early as July 1997 ... months': Antoinette Louw, Mark Shaw, Lala Camerer and Rory Robertshaw, 1998, 'Crime in Johannesburg: Results of a city victim survey', *Monograph* 18, Institute for Security Studies, Pretoria, Chapter 5.

70 'in the United Kingdom ... their payloads': see 'We were Heros' in *The Economist* of 10 February 2007.

74 'a docket analysis of gun crimes ... a three-month period': Altbeker, 1999, *Guns and Public Safety: Gun crime in Alexandra and Bramley*, commissioned by *Gunfree South Africa*.

76 'be the impact of tracker devices': Altbeker. 2005, *Cars and robbers: Has car theft crime prevention worked too well?*, Institute for Security Studies, Pretoria.

76 'as appears to have been the case in the United States': Ayers and Levitt, 'Measuring positive externalities from unobservable victim precaution: An empirical analysis of lojack', *NBER Working Paper 5928*.

77 'strategy used in Boston': David Kennedy, 1998, 'Pulling Levers: Getting Deterrence Right,' *National Institute of Justice Journal*, National Institute of Justice, Washington DC, pp2-8.

81 'Ron Pashcke': Ron Pashcke, 2000, *Conviction rates and other outcomes of crimes reported in eight South African police areas*, South African Law Commission, Pretoria.

82 'the United States maintains a conviction rate for robbery of around 20%, in England and Wales it is well under 10%': Langan and Farrington, 1998, *Crime and Justice in the United States and in England and Wales, 1981-96*, US Department of Justice, Washington DC.

85 'The most authoritative study': Mathews, Abrahams, Martin, Vetten, Van der Merwe and Jewkes, 2005, '*Every six hours a woman is killed by her intimate partner*': *A national study of*

female homicide in South Africa, South African Medical Research Council, Cape Town, p1.

86 'WHO study on violence': Krug, Dahlberg, Mercy, Zwi and Lozano (eds), 2002, *World report on violence and health*, World Health Organisation, Geneva.

88 'Indeed, it wasn't so long ago … authorised the "reasonable chastisement" of an obstreperous wife': Vetten, 'Domestic violence, murder and the law' in *Sunday Independent*, 22 November 1998.

91 'Angela Carter': quoted in Kerrigan, 1996, *Revenge Tragedy: Aeschylus to Armageddon*, Oxford University Press, Oxford, p225.

96 'The textbook account of the roots of present-day violence': SA Government, 1996, *The National Crime Prevention Strategy*, South African Government, Pretoria.

97 'Gary Kynoch': Kynoch, undated, *Urban Violence in Colonial Africa: A Case for South African Exceptionalism*, mimeo; Kynoch, 2005, *We are Fighting the World: A history of the Marahea Gangs in South Africa, 1947-1999*, Ohio University Press, Athens.

101 'Mark Danner': Danner, 2005, *The Massacre at El Mozote: A Parable of the Cold War*, Granta Publications, London, p25.

102 'Even so, its murder rate, estimated in 2002 at 38 per 100 000': World Health Organisation, 2004, *World Health Report 2004: Changing History*, World Health Organisation, Geneva, Statistical annex.

103 'Robert Guest': Guest, 2005, *The Shackled Continent: Africa's Past, Present and Future*, Pan Macmillan, London.

105 'that public expenditure actually ameliorates inequality rather than worsening it': Seekings and Natrass, 2006, *Race, Class and Inequality in South Africa*, University of KwaZulu-Natal Press, Durban.

107 'Nor is it obvious … can be improved by better regulation': for an account of the challenges of policing shebeens, see

Altbeker, 2007, *The Dirty Work of Democracy: A year on the streets with the SAPS*, Chapter Five, Jonathan Ball Publishers, Johannesburg.

107 'Guns are another matter': Altbeker, 2004, 'Guns and public policy' in Dixon and Van der Spuy (eds), *Justice Gained: Crime and Crime Control in South Africa's Transition*, UCT Press, Cape Town, pp58–82.

109 'everyday abnormality': Vladislavic, 2006, *Portrait with keys: Jo'burg and what what*, Umuzi, Johannesburg, p139.

110 'We have about the same number of cops … as the international average': Newman, 1999, *op cit*, and Altbeker, 2005, *Paying for Crime: South African spending on criminal justice*, Institute for Security Studies, Pretoria.

112 'Half-made' is a phrase generally attributed to VS Naipaul and appears in numerous interviews with him.

113 'dance floor at a party': The metaphor of a dance floor draws on Mark Buchanan, 2007, 'Chain reactions' at http://donkeyod.wordpress.com/2007/05/31/chain-reactions/

117 'argument has been used persuasively to explain why crime exploded in America in the mid-1960s': Wilson, 1985, 'Crime amidst plenty' in *Thinking about Crime*, Vintage, New York.

117 'steadily younger': StatsSA, 2006, *Mid-year Population Estimates*, StatsSA, Pretoria.

119 'enticement, or incitement, of peer group prestige': Amis, 'The Age of Horrorism' in *The Observer*, 10 September, 2006.

125 'HG Wells': Wells, 2002, *War of the Worlds*, Modern Library Edition, New York, p1.

131 'SAPS annual report': SAPS, 2006, *Annual Report 2005/06*, SAPS, Pretoria, p56.

133 'one renowned American student of policing': Klockars, 1985, *The Idea of Police*, Sage, Beverly Hills, p115.

134 'New York's experience with zero-tolerance policing': Altbeker, 2005, 'New York vs Jo'burg: similarities are scarce' in *Focus 42*, Helen Suzman Foundation, Johannesburg.

134 'changes the climate within which would-be criminals decide whether or not to break the law': Wilson and Kelling, 'Broken Windows: The police and neighborhood safety' in Wilson, 1995, *On Character*, The AEI Press, Washington DC, pp12-138.

142 'fallen through the floor': Altbeker, 'What are the prisons for?' in *The Weekender*, 7 July 2007.

143 'I toured the country in 1998 talking to detectives': Altbeker, 1998, *Solving Crime: The state of the SAPS Detective Service*, Institute for Security Studies, Pretoria.

145 'prison capacity has lagged behind the growth in the population': Altbeker, 2005, *Paying for Crime, op cit.*

148 '2.5 million people': SAPS, *Annual Report 2004/05*, SAPS, Pretoria

153 'The role that increased imprisonment played in reducing crime in America is much debated by academics': the data come from William Spelman, 2000, 'The limited importance of prison expansion' in Blumstein and Wallman (eds) *The Crime Drop in America*, Cambridge University Press, Cambridge; Levitt, 2004, 'Understanding Why Crime Fell in the 1990s: Four Factors That Explain the Decline and Six That Do Not' in *The Journal of Economic Perspectives,* Vol. 18, No. 1, pp163-190.

153 'growth of prisoner numbers has deepened the poverty of the underclass and fuelled inequality': Deparle, 2007, 'The American Prison Nightmare' in *The New York Review of Books,* Vol. 60, No. 6.

156 'It's about values, stupid!': This chapter owes much to Wilson, 1997, *The Moral Sense*, Free Press, New York.

166 'researchers from the Human Sciences Research Council': Amoateng and Richter, 2003, 'The state of families in South

Africa' in Daniel, Habib and Southall (eds), *State of the Nation: South Africa 2003-2004*, HSRC Press, Pretoria, pp242-267.

170 'Hope or Despair?': This chapter draws heavily on a paper drafted by myself and Eric Pelser, 'Scenarios 2019: Crime in South Africa' that was commissioned for The Presidency's scenario planning processes in June 2007.